A book for
Family Reading

Take Care in the Bath

A book for
Family Reading

TAKE CARE
IN THE BATH

Fifty-two stories that teach biblical truths

Jim Cromarty

 EVANGELICAL PRESS

EVANGELICAL PRESS
Grange Close, Faverdale North Industrial Estate, Darlington, Co. Durham, DL3
0PH, England

First published 1998

British Library Cataloguing in Publication Data available

ISBN 0 85234 417 1

Other titles in this series:

How to cook a crow
The cat's birthday
One that didn't get away

By the same author:

A book for family worship
*King of the Cannibals — the story of John G. Paton, missionary to the New
    Hebrides*
A mighty fortress is our God — the story of Martin Luther

Printed and bound in Great Britain by Creative Print and Design Wales, Ebbw Vale

To my brother John
a preacher of the 'good news' in the Lord Jesus Christ.

Contents

		Page
Preface		9
1.	Take care in the bath (Jude 24-25)	11
2.	A God who doesn't forget (Jeremiah 31:34)	15
3.	Invite someone else to dinner! (Proverbs 8:4-5)	19
4.	The easy way is not always the best way (Matthew 4:10)	23
5.	I'm free at last! (John 8:31)	27
6.	Rock scones! (John 6:35)	30
7.	I won't! (1 Thessalonians 5:14)	34
8.	The second-hand bookshop (Exodus 20:15)	38
9.	The six-million-dollar man! (Ezekiel 11:19)	41
10.	A barren fig tree (Mark 11:22-23)	45
11.	The day of reckoning (Acts 17:30-31)	49
12.	And where did you come from? (Job 1:21)	53
13.	God's Word is not muzzled (Isaiah 55:11)	56
14.	We're all different (1 Corinthians 12:12,14)	60
15.	Unity in the church (1 Corinthians 12:20)	64
16.	He let the side down (Matthew 5:16)	68
17.	The loneliest man in the world (Matthew 27:46)	72
18.	A big dog (Hebrews 13:5)	75
19.	A foolish dog (Psalm 2:4)	79
20.	No clothes (Psalm 32:1-2)	82
21.	He murdered my father! (Matthew 6:12)	85
22.	Ouch, that stings! (1 Corinthians 15:56-57)	88
23.	The first Adam (Genesis 1:27)	91
24.	The last Adam (Luke 2:11)	94
25.	Shipwreck! (Hebrews 2:1)	98
26.	Beware of the wave! (Matthew 24:44)	102
27.	A high tower (Proverbs 18:10)	106
28.	Lest we forget! (1 Corinthians 11:26)	109

29. Branding (John 13:35) 112
30. A big fall (1 Corinthians 10:12) 115
31. The diet is working (2 Corinthians 3:18) 119
32. Thank you for your card (Luke 17:15-16) 122
33. My daddy's in heaven (Romans 8:18) 126
34. Hale-Bopp visits the earth (Revelation 22:20) 130
35. Two ways: the broad way (Jeremiah 21:8) 133
36. Two ways: the narrow way (Deuteronomy 30:19) 136
37. The first birth (Luke 1:13) 140
38. The second birth (John 1:12-13) 143
39. The first death (Genesis 3:19) 146
40. The second death (Revelation 20:14) 150
41. I'm hungry (Psalm 81:10) 153
42. The dog sat on the tucker-box (Deuteronomy 7:9) 156
43. Chasing your tail is a waste of time (Ecclesiastes 12:8) 159
44. He had one good friend (Proverbs 18:24) 162
45. Who is the head of the church? (Ephesians 1:22-23) 165
46. Treasure in pieces of clay (2 Corinthians 4:7) 169
47. Dogs not allowed (Revelation 22:15) 172
48. Don't be a drip! (Proverbs 21:19) 175
49. Kept by grace (2 Corinthians 12:9) 179
50. Beware of the horse! (Ephesians 6:1) 182
51. Don't upset your children! (Ephesians 6:4) 186
52. Christ always first (Mark 8:34) 189

Preface

This is the fourth book to be published in the series 'A Book for Family Reading', with the result that there are now in excess of two hundred Bible-based stories available in this form for families to use with their children.

The old *Shorter Catechism* teaches us that 'Man's chief end is to glorify God and enjoy him for ever.' Let us never forget this great truth! To know God and be united to his Son, the Lord Jesus Christ, is the sovereign work of God — the gracious work of the Holy Spirit bringing about the 'new birth'. Parents have a part to play in God's purposes, as he works through means, and mums and dads may well be the means the Almighty uses to save their children.

One of our great hopes must surely be to see our children coming to a saving knowledge of Christ. The world doesn't want to know about the reality of sin and hell and most people ridicule the Christian teaching of life after death. We live at a time when the vast majority of men and women are unconcerned with eternity and live for the present. And this attitude is constantly hammering away at our children. The world at large is racing towards hell without a care.

Parents, provide a Christian atmosphere in your home, where Christ is glorified and the family is daily gathered together to worship the living God. Pray for your children, read the Scriptures to them and provide Christian reading material that will edify their minds.

May God be pleased to use these books to that end — and may he have all the glory.

Jim Cromarty

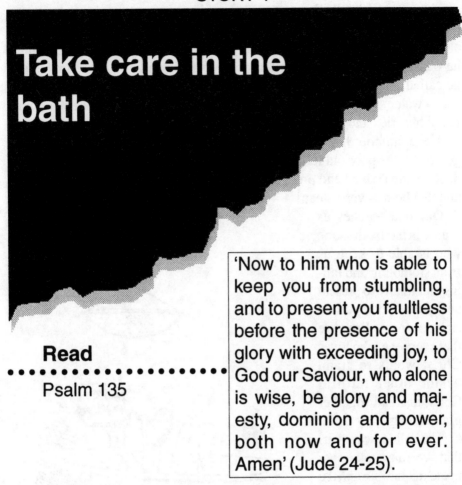

Take care in the bath

Read

• • • • • • • • • • • • • • • • • • • •

Psalm 135

'Now to him who is able to keep you from stumbling, and to present you faultless before the presence of his glory with exceeding joy, to God our Saviour, who alone is wise, be glory and majesty, dominion and power, both now and for ever. Amen' (Jude 24-25).

Learning to walk is a difficult job. I'm sure you have watched a small child learning to stand up and then take that first step. Usually the legs wobble and down the baby goes. But that isn't the end of the matter as almost at once the child pulls himself up again and tries to take another step. When Mum and Dad clap their hands and give a lot of praise, another effort is made and soon the child is walking, and creating problems. He pulls down the things he wants and generally causes a lot of new problems for the family. Usually everyone has to start putting things up higher and higher until the child learns that he must be careful with what is owned by other people.

When people get on in years and old age creeps on they are in danger of falling. Their bones become weak and there is always the real possibility of broken bones if they fall. Many older people begin to make use of a walking stick, or a walking frame, to prevent falls.

A dear old man I knew well had several falls and was very careful when he walked anywhere. He lived by himself and every morning a neighbour called in to make sure he was alive and well. Then in the afternoon another neighbour called at the house to check on him.

One day the elderly man locked the bathroom door, climbed into the bath and started to take a shower. But — yes, he fell over in the bath, and there he was! He was too frail to pull himself up again and no matter how loudly he called for help, no one came. There he stayed in the bath, with lovely warm water spraying over him, for almost two hours before the neighbour heard his cries and came to the rescue.

The neighbour had to break the door open and then, very carefully and gently, lift the poor old fellow out of the bath and help him onto his bed. The doctor soon arrived and pronounced that the man was unhurt in any way — and that he was very clean!

Our text teaches us that Christ is the one who is able to keep us from stumbling and falling and finally to present us before God in perfect righteousness. I'm sure that everyone who loves Christ wants to stand beside other faithful Christians and together praise and glorify God.

The Bible warns us that we must take care not to fall into sin and the time of greatest danger is when we think we are safe and secure. Paul writes, 'Therefore let him who thinks he stands take heed lest he fall' (1 Corinthians 10:12). King David was a godly man, but he stole another man's wife and then had her husband murdered. That was a terrible fall into sin. We learn from that incident that even the greatest Christian can be trapped by Satan.

Today Christians easily fall into sin. They become bad-tempered with each other; some swear; others tell rude stories and watch sinful things on TV. Others are greedy and never seem to be satisfied with what God has given them. Then there are some who never seem to show love to others and always want to have their own way in everything that happens.

When we are tempted to sin, we have a promise from God: 'No temptation has overtaken you except such as is common to man; but God is faithful, who will not allow you to be tempted beyond what you are able, but with the temptation will also make the way of escape, that you may be able to bear it' (1 Corinthians 10:13).

Again and again we are warned in Scripture to avoid 'falling': 'Beware lest you also fall from your own steadfastness, being led away with the error of the wicked' (2 Peter 3:17). God's warning is very plain, as is his promise of help when we do fall.

Every Christian who reads these words knows how easy it is to fall into sin. We need the grace of God to remain faithful. And let us always remember that the power of sin in our lives has been broken — we are new people in Christ. Because of this we can have the victory over sin.

Sometimes we become very worried about our Christian lives because of our sins. We may even question whether we are Christians at all. Let us remember the promise that Christ made to all his people: 'And I give them eternal life, and they shall never perish; neither shall anyone snatch them out of my hand. My Father, who has given them to me, is greater than all; and no one is able to snatch them out of my Father's hand' (John 10:28-29).

So all who belong to Christ are safe and secure. We shall never perish. We may fall into sin, but never fall in such a way that God cannot lift us up. God frequently uses our brothers and sisters in Christ to lift us up, which means that we also have an obligation to fellow Christians when we see them falling into sin. Paul wrote, 'Brethren, if a man is overtaken in any trespass, you who are spiritual restore such a one in a spirit of gentleness, considering yourself lest you also be tempted' (Galatians 6:1). The church must be a group of loving people, ready to mount a rescue operation for any who fall into sin.

One writer — I think it was the great Charles Spurgeon — likened the Christian's fall into sin to a sailor walking about the deck of a ship in rough weather. Many times the sailor was knocked off his feet when huge waves struck the side of the boat, but he was always able to scramble back onto his feet and get on with his work. At no time could he be lost overboard as around the side of the ship there was a safety-rail which prevented people from falling into the sea and drowning.

So, praise God, all who belong to Jesus will one day see him face to face and enjoy his presence for ever. We read in Psalm 135 that the saints will praise God in the temple of the Lord. That is where we shall stand, if we are Christians — with all the saints who make up his 'special treasure'.

We have a wonderful God and our reading describes the power and glory of the one who gave his Son to die upon a cross that we might live. We read in verse 14 of the psalm: 'For the LORD will judge his people, and he will have compassion on his servants.'

God has been good to his people! He judges us in Christ and does not see our sins. 'Praise the Lord!'

To think about

● ●

1. Today's text speaks about 'stumbling'. What is the meaning of the word here?
2. What causes Christians to stumble?
3. What can you do to remain faithful to the Lord Jesus Christ?
4. In the chapter you have read the name of Charles Spurgeon. Who was he?

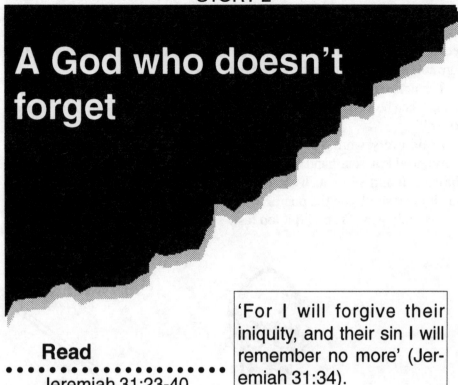

A God who doesn't forget

Read
•••••••••••••••••••
Jeremiah 31:23-40

'For I will forgive their iniquity, and their sin I will remember no more' (Jeremiah 31:34).

Did you ever hear about the man who tied a piece of string around his finger to remind him to buy some flowers for his wife? After arriving at work someone asked him what the string was doing around his finger, and the poor fellow didn't know what to say as he had forgotten why he had put it there! Now I'm sure some of my readers have the problem of a forgetful memory, while other people never seem to forget anything.

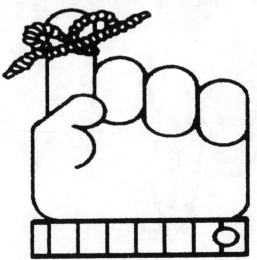

Many years ago when I was at school the teacher gave us homework. We were all to learn the poem 'The Man from Snowy River' by the Australian poet Banjo Paterson. Our teacher was a strict disciplinarian who demanded the very best from each student. In those days the cane was used and all the class were always on their best behaviour.

15

I had been learning the poem for some time and soon knew every word. That night I practised again and again in my bedroom till I could say the whole poem word for word. I wanted to be sure just in case I was asked to recite the poem. As there were about forty-five children in the class I felt sure someone else would be called out.

The next day we all sat quietly as the teacher reminded us of our homework. Then he said, 'Cromarty, out you get and say "The Man from Snowy River"!'

I said every word and was about to sit down when the teacher said, 'Cromarty! Put your hand out!' and with that he gave me two smacks with the cane. It hurt very much and tears came to my eyes as I asked, 'Why did you hit me, sir? I said the poem.'

His reply was: 'You said it too fast!'

Thirty years later at a teachers' conference where I was the guest speaker I was introduced to the very man who had so unjustly caned me. I couldn't resist getting my feelings off my chest — feelings that I had harboured for so long. I could not forget that unjust caning.

'Why did you cane me?' I asked slowly. Then I went on to remind him what had happened, but he said he could not remember the event. Anyhow he said he was never as cruel as I made out. But I still clearly remember the morning when I was caned for saying a poem too fast.

As we read our Bibles we discover that on many occasions God punished his people because of their sinful ways. God hates sin and is angry with all who break his law. He was angry with his people on one occasion and they were taken captive from their homeland into Babylon. But God would never forget his people whom he loved. He had chosen Abraham to be the father of a great nation, a nation that would serve him and from whom Christ would come.

God does not forget his people. At the very time when the Israelites were being punished for their sins by the Babylonians, God said,

Can a woman forget her nursing child,
And not have compassion on the son of her womb?
Surely they may forget,
Yet I will not forget you.
See, I have inscribed you on the palms of my hands...
(Isaiah 49:15-16).

Even as God's people were being taken into captivity they knew that he loved them and one day would bring them home. They also longed for the day when God would make a new covenant with his people: a covenant which was sealed with the blood of the Lord Jesus Christ. Because of his death on the cross as a sacrifice on their behalf, the sins of all his people would be forgiven and the law of God would be written on their hearts and in their minds. This was the law of love — love both towards God and their fellow men and women.

The church of the Old and New Testament days would be one, all serving, worshipping and loving the Lord Jesus Christ and all saved by Jesus Christ through a faith given by God himself.

No, God does not forget his people who trust in the Lord Jesus Christ. He knows us by name and has written our names in his book of life. He has promised to be with us at all times and in all situations of life.

On Judgement Day, he will call us all one by one, using our names, and reward us for our faithfulness to Christ. On that day all his people will hear the wonderful words: 'Well done, good and faithful servant' (Matthew 25:23). God has made a record of all our works, both good and evil — nothing is forgotten. On that day, when Christ is seated upon the throne of judgement, the books will be opened and we shall be judged 'according to [our] works' (Revelation 20:13). All who trust in Christ as their Saviour are pronounced guiltless because Christ has paid the penalty for their sins and he has perfectly obeyed God's law on their behalf. Instead they will receive a reward from the Saviour according to their faithfulness in serving him.

The God who will never forget his people is the same God who, because of the saving work of his Son, has forgiven the sins of his people and will remember them no more.

Reader, if you are a Christian I'm sure that there are times when the remembrance of your sins comes flooding back and you hang your head in shame and godly sorrow. But remember that the blood of our Saviour does indeed cleanse us from all sin (1 John 1:7). Remember that as you are clothed in Christ's perfect righteousness you may enter heaven. In God's eyes he sees you in Christ and that means he sees you as being perfect, just like Jesus.

Let all who live by faith in Christ praise God for his goodness and rejoice in the salvation that cost the life of his Son. Thank God daily for all that he has done for you!

If you are not yet a Christian remember that, unless you come to Christ for forgiveness of your sins, one day you will have to answer to God yourself for all you have done and bear the punishment for them yourself. It will be too late then to call on him for mercy if you have rejected Christ as your Lord and Saviour during your lifetime.

To think about

• •

1. We know that God punishes sinners. Why does he do this?
2. If you are a Christian you will appear perfectly righteous in God's eyes. How can this be?
3. The Jews were taken into captivity by the Babylonians. Why did God punish his people?
4. What does the Bible mean when it tells us that our sins are 'forgiven'?

Invite someone else to dinner!

Read
• • • • • • • • • • • • • • • • • •
Luke 14:15-24

'To you, O men, I call, and my voice is to the sons of men. O you simple ones, understand prudence, and you fools, be of an understanding heart' (Proverbs 8:4-5).

In one of my other books I wrote about some good friends who for several years lived in Penang in Malaysia. Peter worked with the Air Force and was stationed at the Butterworth Air Force Base. He and his wife Judy and son Joshua lived in a spacious apartment in a very tall building overlooking the Straits of Malacca. While they were in Penang we were invited to visit them.

Val and I had a wonderful holiday. We did things and saw places that were so different from anything in Australia. While there I was invited to preach in a Presbyterian church in Penang and also to conduct a baptism.

Not long ago Peter rang and said they were coming to visit us. Val and I were excited as we had not seen Peter and his family for quite a long time.

So Val began to prepare for their visit. Chickens were cooked and other tasty foods were prepared the day before. By doing this we would have more time for talking when our friends arrived.

Then at about 10 a.m. on the day they were to come we had a phone call and I heard Peter, at the other end of the line, say, 'Jim, we won't be coming. We're so upset, but we had an accident and the car has been taken away for repairs.'

No one had been hurt so we thanked God for that, but our visitors could not come. The table was set and the food was ready for eating.

Val asked, 'What are we going to do with all this food?' Then we both remembered the parable told by Christ — the one you have just read.

'Well,' Val suggested, 'we can't eat everything ourselves. Let's ask a few friends in and have a meal together.' And that's what we did.

The parable in today's Bible reading is about an important man who had invited his friends to the wedding of his son. The invitations to the man's friends, which were sent out well in advance of the day, had been accepted, but when the day for the wedding drew near and a reminder was sent they began to make excuses.

'I've just bought some oxen and must make sure they are good workers. I can't come,' said one. Another claimed he had just been married, so how could he come?

Now, none of those excuses was satisfactory, as the people who had accepted the invitations had had plenty of time in which to get themselves organized. Their failure to attend meant that the father of the bridegroom had plenty of food and no one to eat it.

The man was angry when he heard the weak excuses from those he had invited, but he was determined he was going to have people at his son's wedding breakfast! So he sent his servants out into the streets of the city in which he lived to invite the poor, the sick and injured to the wedding feast. These were the ones who would enjoy the feasting.

However, because there were still vacant seats at the wedding reception the servants went out into the highways to find others to bring along to the wedding. Soon the servants had the hall filled with people who celebrated the wedding of the rich man's son to his beautiful bride.

We know that this parable is about our heavenly Father, who sent his servants, the prophets, to his people Israel, inviting them to the marriage of Christ to his bride, the church. It was to the people of Israel that Jesus came, and they turned their backs upon him and eventually killed him by nailing him to a cross.

God's chosen people wanted nothing to do with their promised Messiah, King Jesus, the greatest son of David. So the gospel was taken to the Gentiles — the people despised by the Jews. The nobodies of the world became 'somebodies' in God's eyes, and they too heard the good news of the love of God's Son, the Lord Jesus Christ.

Maybe you live in a family where Mum and Dad love and serve the Lord Jesus Christ. The gospel is offered to you: 'Come to Jesus and confess your sins. He will freely forgive you and make you a new person. Then show your love to him for saving you by serving him all the days of your life.'

And what is your reply? Have you said, 'No, I don't want anything to do with Jesus Christ. I want to live my own life and do as I please'?

If that is your attitude, be warned: the gospel may be taken from you and offered to someone else who will appreciate what Christ has done. They will then learn of God's great love of sinners and will come to love and worship the eternal, living God. But, unless you repent and call on him for mercy before it is too late, when Christ comes at the end of time to gather his people together to be with him, you will find that you have no part in the great wedding feast. Instead you will be shut out of God's presence and separated from all his people for ever.

What is it to be, reader? Will you sit down at the great wedding breakfast when Christ is presented with his bride, the church, made up of all who believe and trust in the Redeemer, the Lord Jesus Christ?

To think about

● ●

1. Today's reading is about a feast. Who were represented by the people who refused to attend the wedding?
2. Who are the Gentiles? Why has the gospel been preached to the Gentiles?
3. What do you think is the teaching of this parable?

The easy way is not always the best way

Read
• • • • • • • • • • • • • • • • • • •
Matthew 4:1-11

> 'Then Jesus said to him, "Away with you, Satan! For it is written, 'You shall worship the LORD your God, and him only you shall serve' " ' (Matthew 4:10).

Jesus Christ came into the world to save sinners. How we should praise God for that glorious work! Without Christ's death upon that accursed cross no one would have been saved.

Today's Scripture reading tells us about the time when Satan confronted Christ in the wilderness. Satan knew that his own kingdom was under attack and his only hope was to cause Christ to sin. He knew that Christ had come into the world to save sinners and this was something he wanted to frustrate, as only he could. So Satan decided to tempt Christ by offering him an easy way to rule the kingdoms of the world. However, the easy way is not always the best way, as most of us know.

Some years ago a friend and I decided to go fishing. We had to drive along a tarred road, park the car in a car park and then walk several miles along the beach to the fishing spot. It was a long walk in the soft sand, with fishing-rods and fishing gear over our shoulders, but we knew it would be worth it all so long as the fish were biting.

As we were driving along my friend suggested we take a short cut. 'I've been along the track many times,' he said. 'It's a sand track through the bush, but if you're careful there will be no problems. And the track ends at the bottom of a sand-hill about 100 metres from the fishing spot.'

23

I didn't like the idea of driving through the bush along a narrow sandy track, but my friend assured me, 'There will be no problems. This is the easy way.'

We found the track which really was a bush track. The wheels spun in the sand and we had to travel very slowly to miss the trees and rocks. After a quarter of an hour we reached a sand-hill probably forty metres high. It wasn't long before we had all our fishing gear at the top of the hill and there, a couple of hundred metres away, was the sea. Yes, this was the easy way to reach the fishing spot!

We fished well into the night and caught many bream. Then came the time to find the car and go home — but where was the car? We had no idea in the darkness where we had parked it. When we reached the top of the sand-hill all we could see was miles of bush. So we started walking back and forwards along the very soft ridge of sand looking for the car. It took us several hours to discover the spot where we had carefully parked it. If we had parked where I had originally intended we would have been home in no time at all. The easy way was proving to be the hard way!

Exhausted, we finally saw the moonlight shining on the roof of the car. Then came the problem of driving back along the sandy track in the bush. It

wasn't long before we were bogged down in the sand. It took an hour or so to dig the car out. None of this would have happened if I had not followed my friend's advice to take the short cut.

We eventually reached home, completely worn out and with scratches on the car where we had brushed against overhanging trees. The short cut, the easy way, had in fact proved to be the difficult way. Never again did we use the short cut!

Satan offered Christ a short cut to world rule. 'Just bow down and worship me and all the kingdoms of the world will be yours,' he said, tempting Christ. But that easy way was not God's way. God's way was the cross by which he would save a people and establish a worldwide kingdom. God's way was the way of obedience.

Christ would never bow down to Satan! To do so would have been sin, and then no one would have been saved. The 'easy' way was the wrong way.

We must all remember this as far as our Christian life is concerned. The Christian life can be very difficult. Today we have people telling us that God will save everyone if they are sincere in what they do and believe. That is the easy way, but it is not God's way. There is no difficulty in living a life of ease that doesn't upset anyone. Recently I received a letter from a person who accused me of teaching falsehood. He claimed that if people just loved one another all would be well, but he objected to keeping God's laws as a way of showing his love of Christ.

Following Christ faithfully is the difficult way. Christ told his disciples that they had to take up the cross and follow him (Matthew 10:38), which means that all who live the life of faith are to be obedient to Christ, exposing the sin of the world and calling people to repentance. It means becoming identified with the humiliation and suffering of Christ. It means a willingness to become an outcast for the sake of the Lord Jesus. Most non-Christians hate those who speak out against sin and they can make life very unpleasant for those who faithfully follow Christ. However, the end of the way of the cross is heaven — eternal joy in the presence of God in Christ. The easy way can be very pleasant, but as we read in Proverbs 14:12, the end of that way is death: 'There is a way that seems right to a man, but its end is the way of death.'

The easy way is not always the best way. Christ chose the way of the cross instead of bowing down to Satan. The way of the cross meant distress, pain and death, but it is because he chose that way that we can be saved and one day will gaze upon the face of our beloved Saviour.

Which pathway are you following? I pray that you will follow the way of the cross — that is, of faith in Christ and faithful service to him, not counting the cost — which leads to eternal life.

To think about

• •

1. Who is Satan?
2. The Lord Jesus Christ is King. How did he become a king and win a kingdom?
3. How do sinners become members of Christ's kingdom?
4. What must we do when tempted by Satan?

I'm free at last!

'Then Jesus said to those Jews who believed him, "If you abide in my word, you are my disciples indeed. And you shall know the truth, and the truth shall make you free"' (John 8:31).

Freedom! We live in a world where people are demanding the right to live as they please. The same was true when Christ was on earth, but he taught the people that true freedom was to be found in him alone. The freedom the world wants is freedom without responsibility, and that type of freedom is licence.

Our dog Wags would love to be free. He has the run of our home. He spends time during the day lying on our bed gazing through the window. When he sees something that attracts his attention he jumps off the bed and then stands on his hind legs to look through the window. He barks at the cats and dogs that go by and I'm sure he longs to be out with those animals that seem to be living a life of freedom.

Wags is able to run around in the garden, but he cannot get through the locked gate or over the fence. He is free to run about, but his freedom has limits to it.

Not long ago some of our grandchildren visited us. Wags loves these young people and when Val opened the front door to let them in, he darted through. He barked at the grandchildren and then turned and ran for the street. He must have thought that he was free at last. He seemed so excited

27

as we called out to him, 'Sit, Wags!' But there was no stopping him. When he saw some cars coming towards him he raced across the road, barking. Then another dog appeared and he turned and ran towards him. I think Wags was looking for an enjoyable game. He was free and appeared to be relishing his freedom.

We stood watching anxiously as Wags raced across the road, just avoiding being knocked down by a car. He had his eyes on the other dog and couldn't see anything else. Eventually we ran him down and put him back in the garden where he was once again safe.

The freedom that Wags wanted almost ended in his death. Now there are so many young people today who want their freedom. They think that if only they can get away from home and Mum and Dad they will be free. They hate the fences that their Mum and Dad have put up to protect them. They long for freedom to do as they please.

However, no one in this world is free. We are all born into this world as slaves to sin. The Bible teaches a great truth: 'There is none righteous, no, not one ... there is none who seeks after God' (Romans 3:10-11). David put it like this: 'Behold, I was brought forth in iniquity, and in sin my mother conceived me' (Psalm 51:5). Yes, until God gives us a saving faith in Christ, we are slaves to sin and members of Satan's kingdom. Even though they may not know it, the freedom non-Christian people want is really the freedom to commit even more sin.

Often young people who long for freedom from the rules of Mum and Dad end up becoming slaves of drugs, alcohol, immorality and a pleasure-seeking lifestyle. They turn away from the law of God and the teachings of their parents, thinking they can live a life of total freedom, but in fact they are plunging deep into slavery.

Many parents today weep tears for their children who have rejected God and are walking a pathway that leads to hell. Many young people come to their senses when it is too late to prevent sin from wreaking havoc in their own lives or those of others. 'If only...' are the sad words they speak as tears flow from their eyes. 'If only...' are the saddest words in the English language. Even though God forgives all those who truly repent of their sins and trust in Christ, the past cannot be undone and the effects of past sin may continue to be felt during the remainder of the believer's life on earth.

Of course no Christian is totally free from sin until he or she passes into the presence of Christ and is made perfectly holy. Yet true freedom is ours when the power of sin is broken. Paul wrote, 'Therefore, if anyone is in Christ, he is a new creation; old things have passed away; behold all things have become new' (2 Corinthians 5:17). Elsewhere Paul tells us that when we belong to Christ sin no longer rules us (Romans 6:14). Now this is real freedom! — freedom from the rule of Satan and freedom to serve and worship God. When the Holy Spirit brings about the new birth the sinner repents of his or her sins and willingly follows Christ.

Our reading is about the Jews who declared that they were 'free'. They claimed that they had never been in 'bondage' to anyone. However, if they only looked around them they would have seen the armed Roman soldiers walking about the streets. They were at that very moment being ruled by Pilate, the Roman governor. If they thought about their history they would have remembered they had been slaves in Egypt in the days of Moses and slaves of Nebuchadnezzar when the nation was taken captive to Babylon. The only Jew who knew true freedom was the one who loved and served God.

Let us all remember that true freedom is only found in Jesus Christ, the Son of God. All who trust in Christ for salvation are no longer slaves to sin, but are true servants of Christ. This is freedom!

The freedom we have in Christ has a protective fence about it, the law of God, and as we obey God's glorious and wonderful law, we find spiritual security and experience peace with God through the Lord Jesus Christ.

To think about

1. People are born into this world 'slaves' to sin. What does this mean?
2. The Bible tells us that when we become Christians we are 'free'. What does this mean?
3. How is it that a Christian is 'free' when he is to be obedient to the commands of God?

Rock scones!

Read
• • • • • • • • • • • • • • • • • • • •
John 6:22-40

'And Jesus said to them, "I am the bread of life. He who comes to me shall never hunger, and he who believes in me shall never thirst" ' (John 6:35).

Most people in this world eat bread. Some people will not eat meat, but I have not heard of anyone saying 'No' to a slice of bread — unless the person is not hungry, or is on a diet! Of course different types of bread are eaten in the various countries of the world. In the Western world we have large loaves of sliced bread, very different from the flat, pancake type of bread eaten in India, which is the type of bread that would have been cooked for the daily meal when Christ was on earth.

Have you ever tried to cook bread? In the early days of Australia's colonization by the British, the bread commonly used was called 'damper'. It

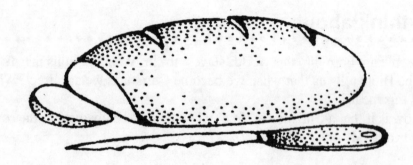

was made from flour, salt and water or milk. Damper was easy to make and lovely to eat, especially when buttered and covered in golden syrup. (In Australia the syrup is called 'cocky's joy'— 'cocky' being the nickname of a farmer!)

Soon after we were married Val and I tried to make some scones. I had no idea how to go about it and Val wasn't too sure either. After a lot of work

and laughter our scones were ready to eat. As I picked one up it was so hot that I dropped it to the floor. To our surprise it bounced like a tennis ball!

Our scones looked like Mum's scones; they smelt like Mum's scones; but they were so solid we threw them all away! Since then we have learned the secret of making scones that are good to eat. Sometimes now we even make bread using yeast.

Bread is an important food worldwide and many people call it the 'staff of life'. In New Testament times bread was so important it was unthinkable that anyone could live without eating bread every day. The people of that age didn't have the wonderful variety of foods we have today.

When the Israelites came out of the land of Egypt, God gave them 'bread from heaven' to eat. This was the 'manna' that the Jews ate in those early days of wandering through the wilderness. They claimed that the 'manna' from heaven was the result of the prayers of their great leader and prophet,

Moses. However, Jesus declared that the 'manna' came from God. It was true that Moses had prayed, but the food came from God, not from Moses.

Then Jesus told his hearers that God had given them the true heavenly bread, which was Christ himself. Here is one of Christ's great 'I AM' statements. By using this expression he was claiming to be God — Jehovah. When God spoke to Moses out of the burning bush, Moses asked who was speaking to him. God's reply was: 'I AM WHO I AM' (Exodus 3:14). We all need to remember that the one who saved us is none other than Jehovah, the eternal God. We have one God who is three persons — Father, Son and Holy Spirit. Our Saviour is Jehovah, the eternal Son.

The Jews had witnessed one of the greatest miracles performed by Christ, the feeding of the five thousand using five barley loaves and two fish. When the stomachs of the listening crowd had been filled they wanted Christ as their king. What a king he would be, they thought, if he could feed them each day with such miraculous food!

However, Christ knew of a greater food that the people needed. This was the true heavenly bread that gave eternal life — Christ himself. The Lord Jesus had come into the world to give his life to save his people. His body would be broken in death and his precious blood would flow from his dying body, so that all who trusted in him might have eternal life.

Jesus was the living bread who had life in himself. All who trust in him are given eternal life. Sinners do not literally eat Christ's body and drink his blood; the very thought of such a thing upset the Jews to whom Christ spoke and many turned away from him as they misunderstood the meaning of his words.

Christ clearly said in our text that 'coming' to him meant spiritual hunger was satisfied. In Matthew we have the words of Christ, spoken to the disciples, where he said, 'Blessed are those who hunger and thirst for righteousness, for they shall be filled' (Matthew 5:6). It is Christ who really satisfies the spiritually hungry sinner. Believing is likened to drinking Christ's blood. So all who want to be saved must go to Christ and rest in him, trusting him for their eternal security.

If you believe in Christ you will need spiritual food day by day, just as you need to eat ordinary food to stay alive and grow. Spiritual food is to be obtained by reading the Bible, reading books which teach biblical truths, meditating on God and on what you have read, speaking to God in your prayers and joining with others in the worship of God. If you do these things you will live and grow spiritually because of the spiritual food you eat.

We have a gracious God who invites sinners to go to Christ and entrust their eternal security to him. Have you done so? If not, then ask God to show you your sins. When you see how you have offended God I'm sure you will want to go to Jesus Christ and seek forgiveness.

To think about

1. What does the word 'manna' mean?
2. Find out all you can about manna.
3. What did Jesus mean when he said he is 'the bread of life'?
4. Explain what is meant by Christ's words: 'Blessed are those who hunger and thirst for righteousness, for they shall be filled' (Matthew 5:6).

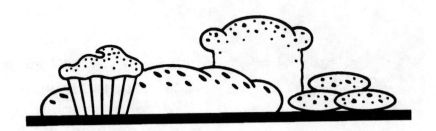

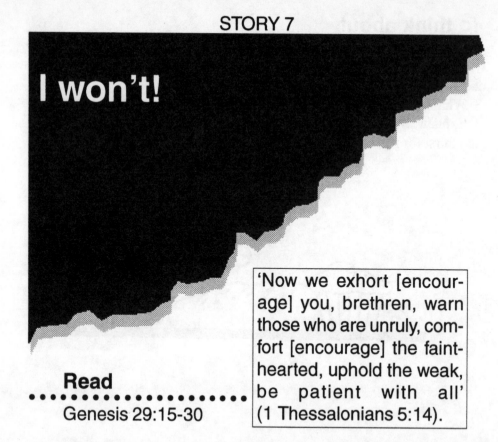

I won't!

Read

Genesis 29:15-30

'Now we exhort [encourage] you, brethren, warn those who are unruly, comfort [encourage] the faint-hearted, uphold the weak, be patient with all' (1 Thessalonians 5:14).

Wags is a dog who knows when to behave himself. If I praise him he will do almost anything for me. If I speak loudly to him he puts his tail between his legs and creeps towards me. If I come towards him with a stick in my hand he sits down almost at once. I have never hit him with a stick, but somehow he knows that sticks can hurt.

Wags likes encouragement. Sometimes when he is on his lead in the garden I turn to take him inside. If he doesn't want to go into the house he just sits down and refuses to walk. If I pull his lead he slides along the grass on his bottom. He refuses to get up and walk. But, if I take a piece of chocolate

out of my pocket he jumps to his feet and trots after me knowing that he will be rewarded for doing the right thing!

Donkeys are well known for their stubborn nature. Often they need encouragement to do what their owner expects of them. Our humorous illustration shows the wisdom of the donkey rider in encouraging his donkey to walk along swiftly. I only hope that when they reached their destination he gave his donkey the carrot! Encouragement without reward is not true encouragement.

Everyone likes to be encouraged and this applies not only to most animals, but to humans as well. Val is encouraged when she is told that she is a good cook and keeps a tidy house. I am encouraged to work on if someone tells me he appreciates what I do. Yes, I'm sure everyone likes to be given a pat on the back now and again.

Our text tells us that mature Christians are to encourage timid and faint-hearted Christians who may at times doubt that their faith really is a saving faith. They may see their sins and wonder if God has really forgiven them. These are the Christians who need our support. We can help them by reminding them of the grace of God and the wonderful promises he has made to all who trust in Christ for salvation.

We can also encourage them by speaking of the glory that awaits all who trust in Christ. What a thrill it is to talk about the goodness of God, who has saved us through the death of his Son on the cross in our place! We can talk to them about the wonder of heaven. This is a real encouragement for the downcast and faint-hearted Christian. We must tell these people to take their eyes off themselves and look to Christ, because that will strengthen their faith. We should also be encouraged in our Christian lives by consider-

35

ing all that Christ has done for us and all that is awaiting us when we leave this world and pass into glory.

When, in the Garden of Gethsemane, Christ faced the reality of his coming death on the cross, he was very downcast and cried out to his Father, 'O my Father, if it is possible, let this cup pass from me; nevertheless, not as I will, but as you will' (Matthew 26:39). Jesus was being crushed by the weight of his people's sins. He knew a horrible death awaited him and sensed that the Father was about to forsake him. God encouraged his Son to face with confidence what lay before him by sending an angel to the garden where he prayed. That angel encouraged and strengthened Christ. Jesus was also encouraged to face death because he knew that through death he would save his people (Hebrews 2:9-10).

Our reading today is about Jacob, who was forced to run away from home to escape his brother Esau, whom he had treated so badly. It was in Haran that Jacob met Laban's daughters and fell in love with the beautiful Rachel. When he asked Laban for the hand of Rachel in marriage he promised to work for seven years to earn his bride. What an encouragement to work on! At the end of the seven years Jacob expected to be given Rachel as his wife. You know the story of how Laban tricked Jacob by giving him Leah instead of Rachel. However, Jacob loved Rachel dearly and was prepared to work another seven years in return for marrying her. Rachel was the encouragement for all Jacob's labour.

Our text then reminds us that if we are Christians we are to encourage our brothers and sisters in Christ. We are also to encourage sinners to turn to Christ for salvation, which means we bear witness to them of God's love. We will be kind to all and ever ready to help people in their need. We will invite sinners to hear the gospel, speaking to them about sin and the wonderful Saviour who died to save his people. We will tell them of the glory that awaits them if they come to Christ and trust in him. We will also warn them that if they do not repent of their sins then hell awaits them.

And those of us who are parents are to encourage our children to follow Christ. We are to train and teach them in the ways of Christ, always remembering the words of the apostle Paul, 'Fathers, do not provoke your children to wrath...' (Ephesians 6:4). We are to love our children and only use punishment as a last resort. We are to set our families an example of godly living.

I remember reading in one of Spurgeon's books about an occasion when he visited a Sunday School. There he asked the children if they wanted to go to heaven. All but one boy said 'Yes'. Spurgeon then asked the boy who said 'No' why he didn't want to go to heaven.

The young fellow replied, 'I don't want to go to heaven because grandfather will be there.' Grandfather, who professed to be a Christian, was not encouraging his grandson to follow Christ. He must have been a hard, unkind man and the boy didn't want to be where his grandfather could continue to show him unkindness.

We are to encourage our children and others to follow Christ. Parents, are you playing your part in this glorious work?

To think about

1. Why do we all need to be encouraged every now and again?
2. Which is the best encouragement you receive from Mum and Dad?
3. How does God encourage his people?
4. What can you do to encourage your parents and others who care for you?
5. Do you ever encourage your hard-working pastor in all the work he carries out? How?

The second-hand bookshop

Read
••••••••••••••••••••
Malachi 3:8-12

'You shall not steal'
(Exodus 20:15).

We live in a world where our possessions are not safe. We often hear of someone whose house has been broken into and goods stolen. In one of my other books I wrote about a girl who broke into our home and stole money.

Some time ago a member of my congregation came to me and asked if I had a copy of a book with the title *Billy Sunday*. All I could say was that I once had a book by that name, but, sad to say, I had no idea where it was. I knew that someone had borrowed the book some years before and it had never been returned. I was disappointed as it was a special book about a most unusual Christian.

The lady smiled and then asked me, 'Would you like your book back again?'

When I asked, 'Do you know where it is?' she put her hand into the bag hanging from her shoulder and produced my long-lost book.

'Where did you find it?' I asked. I knew she had not borrowed it and was amazed that she now had it with her.

'I was looking through a second-hand bookshop and there I found this book with your name in it,' she replied.

I took my book, thanked her for returning it and then paid her the $1.00 she had paid for it. My name was in the book and there beside it was another

name which I could hardly read. It had been written in pencil and was almost rubbed out. When I worked out the name I knew who had borrowed my book and sold it to the second-hand dealer. That was theft! The person involved had sold something that belonged to someone else. That person had sold my book!

Then I began to think about the books in my library and decided I should check them out in case I had a book belonging to someone else. Sure enough, there on a shelf I discovered a book with the name of a friend clearly visible. I then returned the book and was told that I had had the book for about five years. I was very embarrassed.

I guess many, if not all, of us are guilty at some time or another of taking or keeping for ourselves something which does not belong to us. All that is stealing and is sinful. Some people cheat on their taxes; some don't pay their bills; some children even steal money from their parents, and too many people steal from God.

In our Bible reading Malachi accused the Jews of stealing from God by not giving their tithes — that is, one tenth of their income. They had not brought to the temple priests the best animals for sacrifice. They had been giving God anything but the best. Malachi asked the Jews to put God to the test. He told them to pay their tithes and then God would bless them beyond their wildest dreams because God is no person's debtor.

In Acts 5:1-11 you can read about two people who stole from God. They sold their property and then claimed they had given all the proceeds to the church. They could have kept all the money for themselves without sinning if they had been honest about it, but by keeping a portion for themselves while claiming they had given all to the church they were thieves as well as liars. In effect they stole from God. God then punished these two, Ananias and Sapphira, by striking them down dead.

I wonder if any of my readers are guilty of stealing from God. Do you give to the work of the Lord in a responsible way? God gave his Son to save his people and gives blessings upon blessings. We who are saved by the work of Christ owe God everything. We must give to God an offering from our income, time and energy.

Stealing is sinful and God does not tolerate sin of any kind. May each one of us be faithful in supporting the work of the church that the gospel might be spread throughout the community in which we live. Maybe we all should check our bookshelves and make sure we have only our own books on them!

To think about

1. What are the Ten Commandments?
2. Make a list of as many ways as you can think of that people are guilty of stealing from others.
3. Why is stealing wrong?
4. When anyone repents of the sin of stealing, what should he or she do?

The six-million-dollar man!

Read
• • • • • • • • • • • • • • • • • • • •
John 1:1-13

'I will put a new spirit within them, and take the stony heart out of their flesh, and give them a heart of flesh' (Ezekiel 11:19).

I'm sure that some of my readers will remember a TV show called *The six-million-dollar man*. As far as I can remember, some doctors had rebuilt a man after an accident. With his new legs he could run like the wind and had great strength.

At the time I thought it was a little far-fetched, but as the years have passed I'm not so sure any more. We live in an age where body parts are being replaced simply and easily. A schoolteacher friend told me he has had two hip replacements and now plays golf and bowls without any aches and pains.

41

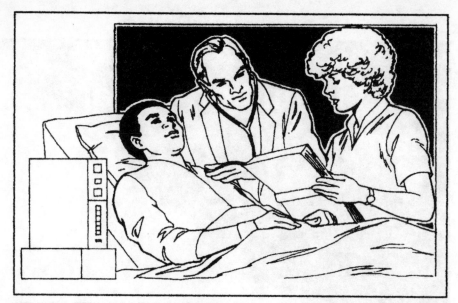

Wonderful things are being done by doctors. Many people have had lenses in their eyes replaced or kidneys transplanted, and we could go on and on. We all know people who have had heart-repair surgery and some of you may know someone who has had a heart transplant. In Australia one delightful young lady has had heart replacement surgery twice. She is well now and works for the Heart Foundation, encouraging people to eat the right food and to exercise, which helps prevent heart disease.

The Bible has a lot to say about the human heart — not the muscle that pumps blood through the body, but the part of us where we have all our feelings. We talk about people being heart-broken and know that this is a feeling of terrible sadness. Yes, we often literally feel it in the chest and sometimes our feelings, of excitement or fear, make the heart beat faster.

The Bible describes the heart as the very centre of our life. By nature the human heart is very sick because it is tainted with sin, which affects every part of us. It was the prophet Jeremiah, speaking God's words, who said, 'The heart is deceitful above all things, and desperately wicked; who can know it?' (Jeremiah 17:9).

Matthew 15:1-20 records the incident where the Pharisee complained to Jesus that his disciples didn't wash their hands before eating. The Pharisees were concerned that some dust from a Gentile might have blown onto the disciples' hands as they walked about. If they swallowed a speck of that dust while eating, they would have become ceremonially unclean.

Jesus told them plainly that it was not what went into the body that defiled someone because every part of that person was already ruined by sin. Jesus said, 'But those things which proceed out of the mouth come from the heart, and they defile a man. For out of the heart proceed evil thoughts, murders, adulteries, fornications, thefts, false witness, blasphemies. These are the things which defile a man...' (Matthew 15:18-20).

Sinners need a new heart and that is what God promised in our text! The day would come when each of his people would receive a spiritual heart transplant. This would be the work of God's Holy Spirit, who would remove the cold, hard, sinful heart and replace it by a soft heart of flesh. This new heart would have God's law written on it and God would be able to mould it in such a way that the person would love to lead a life that was pleasing to God.

Jesus told Nicodemus that he had to be 'born again' (John 3:3), and the apostle John has written that this is the work of God (John 1:12-13; 3:5-8).

We don't inherit the new heart that we need from our godly parents. We don't acquire a heart that loves God because we say we want it, or because the minister and elders say we must have it. Having a heart transplant in a hospital doesn't give you a heart that loves Christ. Only God can give you such a new heart. The Holy Spirit comes and makes the change, taking away the old heart that loves sin and replacing it with a heart that loves God and wants to please him. The new birth is the work of God alone!

So you will never really be able to turn away from sin and live a life pleasing to God unless God changes your heart. The old, sinful heart with which we are all born loves sin. It is the new heart which God gives to all those who are born again that loves God and enables us to live a life of holiness. When God changes your heart you will love him and confess your sins to him, asking his forgiveness. You will hate sin and want to live in a way that is pleasing to God. God's law will be your delight and you will look forward to the time when you will be away from this world of sin and death and will be present with Christ, 'which is far better' (Philippians 1:23). With your new heart you will be a new person.

One Lord's Day I was travelling to the evening worship service, accompanied by two friends. They had been with me to the two earlier services. Suddenly one burst out laughing. I asked Graham what was so funny. He looked at both of us and said, 'I find it hard to believe that Donald and I have attended two services today and we are both looking forward to the next. Six months ago I would not have attended one service.'

A wonderful event had happened in the life of both these men within the last few months. They had been 'born again'. They now loved the Lord and enjoyed worshipping him. Today Graham is a pastor of his own congregation and God is blessing his labours.

Are you a Christian? If not, then pray that God will save you, because of the death of the Lord Jesus for sinners, and give you a new heart. Then you will become a new person and a true servant of the Lord Jesus Christ. And, as a member of his kingdom, you will one day inherit the new creation he is preparing for his people.

To think about

· ·

1. Who were the Pharisees and why did they dislike the Lord Jesus?
2. What did Jesus mean when he said, 'You must be born again'?
3. What changes take place in a person's life when he or she is 'born again'?

A barren fig tree

Read
• • • • • • • • • • • • • • • • • •
Mark 11:12-24

> 'So Jesus answered and said to them, "Have faith in God. For assuredly, I say to you, whoever says to this mountain, 'Be removed and be cast into the sea,' and does not doubt in his heart, but believes that those things he says will be done, he will have whatever he says" ' (Mark 11:22-23).

Hypocrisy is a terrible sin! It is pretending to be something you are not. In my fishing days my brother John and I would tow our boat past what looked like a house built of brick. After several trips we discovered that what we thought was a brick house was in fact a wooden house with a bricked front. The house wasn't what it appeared to be.

There are people today who pretend they are Christians, but this is only on Sunday when they mix with the church people; on Monday and for the rest of the week they live a life that is no different from that of the worldly people about them. They have no difficulty in swearing and speaking in a sinful manner. They even steal when they get the opportunity. All this proves that they are not Christians at all. They pretend to be Christians on Sunday when they are mixing with God's people. Yes, they are hypocrites.

Today's Bible reading is about Christ's meeting with a 'hypocritical' fig tree. The fig tree had all the appearances of having edible fruit, but when

45

Christ and the disciples came to pick and eat the fruit they found it to be bare.

I have read that the fig trees in the Middle East have two differing types of figs. There are the *'baakoor'* figs, which are the early ones found on the tree in springtime. The figs which did not ripen till summer were known as *'kirmoos'*. The early figs normally appeared on the tree before the green leaves were to be found. Plenty of leaves usually meant a crop of them, ripe enough to eat. So when Christ saw leaves on the fig tree he expected to find the sweet *'baakoor'* figs ready for eating. But when he and his disciples reached the tree no figs could be found at all, only green leaves.

Jesus then cursed the tree, pronouncing its death sentence: 'Let no one eat fruit from you ever again!' (Mark 11:14). The Scriptures clearly record that Jesus said those words loudly for the disciples to hear.

Before Christ and the disciples passed that way again they visited the temple where Jesus drove out the money-changers and all those involved in the sale of animals and birds used in sacrifice. The great temple court had become a stockyard. It would have been a stinking mess. This was the second time that Christ had driven from the temple those who desecrated the holy place. This reminds us of the prophecy recorded in Psalm 69:9 where we read: 'Because zeal for your house has eaten me up, and the reproaches of those who reproach you have fallen on me…' Jesus preached to the people that day, taking as his text: 'Is it not written, "My house shall be called a house of prayer for all nations"? But you have made it a "den of thieves"' (Mark 11:17; see also Jeremiah 7:11).

It was on the following day that Christ and the disciples passed the fig tree which Jesus had cursed and Peter saw at once that the tree was already dead. The tree was useless and deserved to be destroyed.

Jesus then spoke to the disciples concerning faith. This was not the ordinary saving faith which all believers have in the Lord Jesus Christ, but that special faith by which the apostles and disciples did great things. Christ spoke of the faith which produced miracles. Paul was referring to this faith when he wrote, 'And though I have all faith, so that I could remove mountains, but have not love, I am nothing' (1 Corinthians 13:2).

Elsewhere Jesus said, 'Many will say to me in that day, "Lord, Lord, have we not prophesied in your name, cast out demons in your name, and done many wonders in your name?" And then I will declare to them, "I never knew you; depart from me, you who practise lawlessness!"' (Matthew 7:22-23).

Great miracles were performed by the apostles. At times they were filled with that tremendous miraculous faith which produced miracles through the power of Christ. Do you remember the crippled man at the temple gate? Peter had probably seen that man lying there many times, but on the day we read of in Acts 3:1-10 he was filled with an overwhelming faith in the healing power of God that resulted in the man being healed.

But false prophets were also capable of performing what appeared to be miracles.

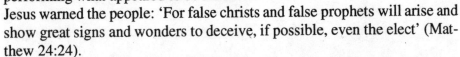

Jesus warned the people: 'For false christs and false prophets will arise and show great signs and wonders to deceive, if possible, even the elect' (Matthew 24:24).

We know that the apostles did great miracles in the name and by the power of Christ during those early days of the Christian church. Miracles still occur, but the days of the public miracles confirming the truth or bearing testimony to Christ are ended.

The fig tree spoke of Israel, God's covenant nation. Jesus came to God's special people, the Jews, who should have been living godly, righteous lives of love and faith — obedient to God's Word. On the outside all looked well, but inwardly the nation was corrupt. People lived for themselves and the world. God was far from their thoughts and this was shown when the Jews crucified God's Son.

The vast majority of the Jews were like that fig tree — all looked well, but the fruits of righteousness were not to be found. Just as the fig tree was cursed and died, so also Israel was placed under God's curse. The judgement of God fell upon the nation when in A.D. 70 the Romans destroyed the temple and the city of Jerusalem.

May each one of us have a strong faith centred upon the Lord Jesus Christ and his saving work! And may there be no hypocrisy found in our lives! God hates hypocrisy! May God bless you all.

To think about

●●●

1. What is a 'hypocrite'?
2. How do we know if a person is a Christian or not?
3. What is meant when we speak of a person having 'saving faith in Jesus Christ'?

The day of reckoning

Read
Joel 3:9-17

'God ... now commands all men everywhere to repent, because he has appointed a day on which he will judge the world in righteousness by the Man whom he has ordained...' (Acts 17:30-31).

'There'll be a day of reckoning!' were words my dad used to say to John and me quite frequently — especially when we were not doing what we should.

The most disturbing days of reckoning I faced as a young boy were school examinations. In my school-days we had to learn our spelling and tables, and no excuses were acceptable for failing to know those facts by heart. We also had to learn and recite poetry, as I mentioned in an earlier chapter.

At the end of each year we faced examinations. The results of those exams were sent in a sealed envelope to our parents so that they would know whether we really knew our schoolwork or not.

The final exams at secondary school were stressful in themselves, but worse still was the fact that our results were published in the newspaper. On a set day we had to buy the daily paper and there, for everyone to see, were our examination results. That really was a day of reckoning.

Some years ago, when I was a schoolteacher, I wanted a promotion. This meant two inspectors visited the school where I taught and carefully examined all that I had done. Later they made a decision concerning my future. That was another time of reckoning.

We all face many days of reckoning during our lives.

As we read the Bible we find that people and nations also had their days of reckoning. Proud, sinful nations and people have been overthrown. In the Old Testament we read of the overthrow of Babylon because of sin. Where is Babylon today? Sodom and Gomorrah had their day of reckoning. The sin of the people of those cities became a stench in the nostrils of God. Today those cities are gone.

Our text reminds us that there is a day of reckoning for all — that day when Christ returns. No one can escape meeting Christ, the Judge. Every man, woman, boy and girl who has ever lived will appear, one by one, before the judgement-seat of King Jesus to receive what God has prepared for him or her. For many people this will be a terrible day! Some people will be praised and rewarded by Christ, while others will be cast into eternal hell because they have loved their sins and rejected God's call to repentance.

Our reading from Joel speaks of that day of reckoning when the nations are called to prepare for battle with Almighty God because he has come in judgement. The world is called together in the 'valley of decision', which is the place where God delivers his decision concerning the eternal status of every individual.

On that day we each will have to give an account of our life — our thoughts, words and deeds — but really the only thing that matters is our relationship to the one who sits upon the judgement-seat. When God 'roars out of Zion' those who have never put their faith and trust in Christ will tremble in fear because they will know that their situation is hopeless and that the open mouth of hell awaits them. What a shocking situation in which to be!

There will be others, however, who will know that all is well with them. They will have the assurance that their sins are forgiven and, because of Christ's saving work, God is not angry with them. In fact their confidence will be based on the fact that Jesus Christ, the great Judge, is none other than Jesus Christ, their Saviour. In Joel 3:16 we read that on that day, 'The LORD will be a shelter for his people.' The Judge is the very one who protects believers from his anger.

Humanity will be divided into two groups: the 'sheep' and the 'goats'— those who are saved by Christ and those who are lost. Then all who belong to Christ, his 'sheep', will hear those wonderful words: 'Come, you blessed of my Father, inherit the kingdom prepared for you from the foundation of the world...' (Matthew 25:34).

Everyone who reads these words will have no excuse on Judgement Day because at this very moment you are called to repentance and faith in Jesus Christ. This is the only way to prepare for God's day of reckoning. Christ invites sinners to turn to him and find forgiveness and eternal salvation. Where do you stand? Do you know Christ as your Lord and Saviour?

To think about

· ·

1. Talk about Judgement Day. What will happen at that time?
2. Who will be God's Judge on that day?
3. In this chapter mention is made of the 'sheep and the goats'. To whom was Christ referring when he used those expressions?

And where did you come from?

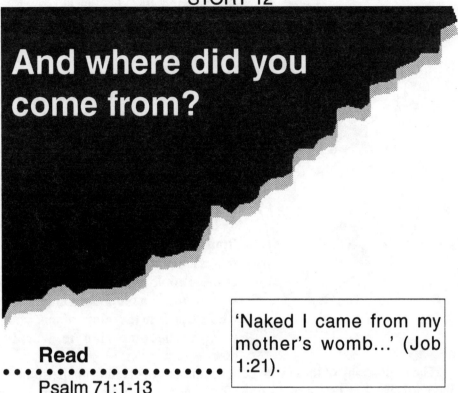

Read
• • • • • • • • • • • • • • • • • • •
Psalm 71:1-13

'Naked I came from my mother's womb...' (Job 1:21).

We live in a world where the majority of people have no real idea where they came from, or where they are going. Few believe in the truth taught in Genesis, and many young people have little real understanding of true family life. Each day they get out of bed with the basic thought: 'What can I do today to enjoy myself?'

I can still remember a child at school telling me that his parents found him in a garden amongst some cabbages. I thought to myself: 'What a shock he is in for one day!' So many parents are unwilling to tell their children 'the facts of life'. Yes, they teach their children their mathematical tables, spelling and other important facts, but not the 'facts of life'.

But worse than that, they never bother telling their children that all mankind came from a loving Creator. The reason why this important fact is not

53

taught is that most parents have no idea of the 'facts of life' concerning human existence. When people do not know where they have come from they usually have no idea where they are going.

My dog has more sense than some people. Wags knows where he lives. As we drive along in the car he starts yelping when we are close to our home. He jumps out of the car when we reach the garage and runs for the front door, as he knows that he lives in our home.

It doesn't matter where people come from in this world as most live for themselves and the pleasure they can get out of life. People who are wealthy usually want to make more money and people who are poor in the things of this world want to become rich in worldly possessions.

The philosophy of those who believe humans evolved from the slime of the earth is: 'Let us eat and drink, for tomorrow we die' (1 Corinthians 15:32). If we did evolve from the earth I think that would be a sound philosophy. If a short seventy years or so is all life is, then we may as well enjoy it to the full. If all we have is seventy or eighty years then our existence is a big joke and has no value at all. It would mean that everything we have worked for during our lives is left behind and lost. After we are dead our children may well take all the things we loved and worked for and throw them onto the rubbish heap.

But I know who created me! Do you? I believe the Bible is the revelation of the living God, who created the world and all things, including humans. One lady who proofread this story commented here, 'My ancestors didn't swing by their tails, but by their necks!' She must have meant she had some ancestors who were executed as criminals, but she knows the truth concerning God's creation of all things. God created men and women to enjoy the creation and to worship and praise him.

The Bible has revealed to me what I am like and what life is all about. I was not placed on this earth to live for myself and get as much out of the world as I can. Every human being is here to appreciate God and glorify him for all that he has done. We are here to enjoy what God has created. We are here to praise God and worship his Son, the Lord Jesus Christ.

Life does not end with our physical death because our spirits live for ever. Just as we all came from the hand of a Creator God, at death every soul returns to the God who created us, the Judge of all mankind. The most important thing in life is not to have our table loaded with the most delicious foods, or to have the best car in our garage, or the biggest bank balance, but to be right with God. If we must one day meet God as a Judge, then surely we want him to meet us as a friend.

Friendship with God is totally dependent upon our relationship with his Son, Jesus Christ. Abraham lived the life of faith in the living God and was called a friend of God. Jesus said to all who love him, 'You are my friends if you do whatever I command you' (John 15:14).

Faith in Christ and a life of obedience to God are the marks of one who is a friend of God. All who know the Lord Jesus as their Saviour and seek to live in obedience to his Word know what life is all about — where they came from and where they are going. God's people are on their way to glory — heaven.

In Psalm 71 we find that the psalmist knew very well that he came from the womb of his mother, but he also knew that God was his Creator and the one who cared for him all the days of his life and would continue to do so into eternity.

Sad to say, there are many people in this world who do not know that their way of life leads to hell. Time is running out for each one of us. We cannot afford to waste time living for the things of the world when important matters are left unattended. Open your Bible, read it and pray to God, confessing your sin and asking him to forgive you because of Christ's sacrifice on the cross. Then go on to show your love and gratitude to the Lord Jesus by obeying his commands.

To think about

• •

1. What happens to a person's soul when death occurs?
2. When will the souls of those who have died be reunited with their bodies?
3. Where did the human race come from?

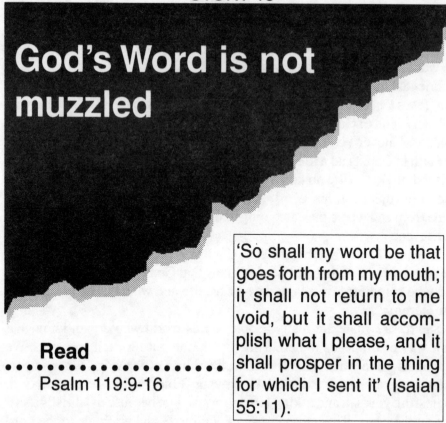

God's Word is not muzzled

Read
• • • • • • • • • • • • • • • • • • • •
Psalm 119:9-16

'So shall my word be that goes forth from my mouth; it shall not return to me void, but it shall accomplish what I please, and it shall prosper in the thing for which I sent it' (Isaiah 55:11).

God's Word is all-powerful, and as our text tells us, it will always accomplish exactly what God intended.

God has a witness to himself in this world and if you have a look at creation — the mountains, the stars, the grass — and then look at yourself in the mirror, your mind will tell you that someone had to be responsible for all that you see. The world in which we live must have had a maker. So the creation bears witness to the Creator.

The creation tells us that our Creator God is almighty, wise and loving. However, looking at the creation does not tell us that we are sinners who need a Saviour. Nor does the creation tell us of the saving work of the Lord Jesus Christ.

God sent his prophets into the world to reveal the good news of the coming Saviour. These men wrote down his message, and today in the Bible we still have the words spoken by the prophets of old.

Two thousand years ago God showed us what he is really like when he sent his Son, the Lord Jesus Christ, into the world. It is in Jesus Christ that we know what God's character is like. The apostle Paul wrote of Christ: 'For in him dwells all the fulness of the Godhead bodily' (Colossians 2:9). Truly, Jesus Christ is God in the flesh.

When we read the New Testament we learn more and more about the wonderful salvation to be found in Christ.

Now God has a people in this world who must hear the word, and this word is found in the book called the Bible. By the sacrificial giving of Christians and the work of Christian organizations the Bible has been translated into most languages of the world, and now is to be found in the vast majority of countries. However, some governments do not want Bibles coming into their countries because they do not want their citizens to follow Christ. One of these countries is communist China, which puts strict limits on the number of Bibles that can be printed and circulated amongst its people.

A friend of mine told me the story of his visit to communist China. Alasdair, the governor of a prison for young criminals, had been invited to visit mainland China and explain some of the methods he was using to help rehabilitate young people who had been in trouble with the law.

Alasdair was also a very active member of Gideons International, an organization responsible for placing Bibles in motels, hotels, hospitals and schools. So he decided to take several suitcases of Bibles with him when he visited China, intending to give a Bible to anyone who would take it from him. However, he was deeply concerned that the Chinese customs officials would confiscate his Bibles before he could give them to anyone. He and many other Christians had prayed long and fervently that God would somehow order events so that Alasdair and his load of Bibles could enter the nation without any difficulties.

After a long flight, he found himself in the Chinese customs department, lined up with many other people who were having their bags examined by the immigration officials. Silently Alasdair prayed that the customs official would somehow allow him to pass through with his Bibles. His turn had almost arrived when he would have to unlock his bags. He thought he would lose his Bibles, when suddenly several soldiers accompanying an important-looking official entered the airport. One of the men announced: 'Mr ....! Mr ...!'

The man was calling Alasdair's name. As soon as he raised his hand and called out, 'Over here!' two soldiers immediately came to his side, carefully took his suitcases and said, 'Follow us!' Then he was escorted to the officials who had arrived with the soldiers.

'Welcome Mr ...! We are here to escort you to your hotel. Welcome to China!' they said as they bowed their heads and shook his hand. Then God had the soldiers carry the precious Bibles into their nation unaware of what they were doing. Everyone moved to the waiting cars and there was Alasdair, safely in communist China with his precious load of Bibles intact.

He learned from this experience that God does rule the affairs of this world. The officials and soldiers arrived just in time! He was able to give the Bibles he carried to many Chinese officials, all of whom gladly accepted them and thanked him sincerely for the gift.

God's purposes were being fulfilled and now his Word was in the hands of many important Chinese officials. In eternity we may well learn of some who were saved through the reading of God's Word carried into China by Alasdair.

At times we think that what we do for Christ is of little use. Putting a tract in a letter-box, or openly carrying a Bible when we go to church on Sunday, may be one step in winning someone to faith in Christ.

Our reading speaks of the wonder of God's Word which the psalmist had hidden in his heart (Psalm 119:11). He loved that Word and learned it by heart. Then he sought to live his life according to the law of the God he loved. Yes, there were times when he fell into terrible sin, but David repented when he realized how he had offended God.

I certainly pray that you might love God's Word, and the one who gave us that Word, God himself! If you are a Christian you will love Christ, and the words found in the Bible will be precious to you.

Maybe you will never have a chance to take Bibles to China, but you will have the opportunity to support those who do take Bibles to all the nations of the world. Do all you can to win people to Christ!

To think about

1. Why are so many people opposed to the teachings of the Scriptures?
2. Who is the Lord Jesus Christ?
3. Find out something about the work of the Gideons.
4. What can you do to spread the good news concerning the Lord Jesus Christ?

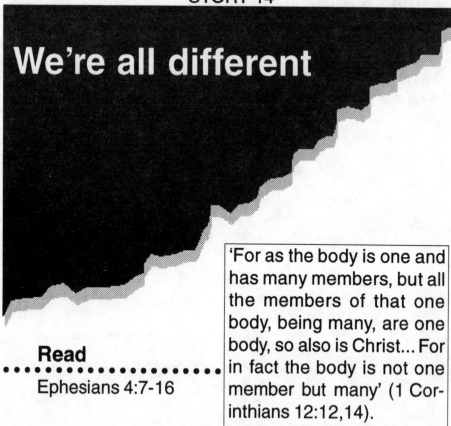

We're all different

Read
• • • • • • • • • • • • • • • • • • • •
Ephesians 4:7-16

'For as the body is one and has many members, but all the members of that one body, being many, are one body, so also is Christ... For in fact the body is not one member but many' (1 Corinthians 12:12,14).

As we look around us we see so many different things. There are hundreds of trees and flowers in various shapes and colours. We see hills, rivers, clouds, the sun, moon and stars. The world is filled with a vast variety of colours — there is so much diversity!

No two people are the same. When I visited Hong Kong everyone looked alike to me. I asked a Chinese shopkeeper if all the white-skinned people who visited her shop looked alike to her and she said, 'Yes, you people are all the same!' But we are all different in so many ways. We have different looks and differing likes and dislikes.

When our children were at home they all had different tastes when it came to food. In one of my other books I wrote about my love of oysters, yet I am the only one in our family who enjoys them. The others just don't know what they are missing! One of the girls didn't like peas, a couple of us didn't like pumpkin and Val had no liking for beetroot. We all lived together and tolerated our differences. When mealtimes came round Valerie knew our likes and dislikes, and while we tried to encourage the children to develop a liking for all foods, eventually she gave each girl just what she liked to eat. Of course, Val didn't bother putting pumpkin on my plate!

One of our daughters was extremely tidy in her bedroom while the others were not so tidy. We are all different. Val likes everything in its place, but knows that my study is usually out of bounds. I have my books and bits of paper spread about everywhere and know where everything is. So Val tolerates the untidiness of my study, even though I know she sneaks in at times and tries to clear the floor as she vacuums.

The church is like a family because every member is different. Last Sunday I paid particular attention to the people who had gathered for worship. There were men and women, boys and girls. Some were getting on in years and others were just babies — and there were some from all ages in between. Some of the men wore suits while others were more casually dressed. Some church members carried out important jobs while others had no particular job at all. I could go on and write of lots of differences which could be seen.

But we all sat together and worshipped God. After the service, we talked with one another and looked forward to meeting again for prayer and Bible study during the week. We know we differ from each other, but we tolerate and appreciate each other's differences. In fact we cannot do without one another. We are like the human body which needs all its parts in order to function properly (1 Corinthians 12:14-19).

Sad to say, every now and again there can be a falling out between Christians. When this happens they must put things right for the sake of their brothers and sisters in Christ. We must all understand that none of us can boast about our abilities, nor can anyone be jealous of another's capabilities, because God has made us the way we are. He placed us in our situation in life. We read the apostle Paul's words in 1 Corinthians 4:7: 'For who makes you differ from another? And what do you have that you did not receive? Now if you did indeed receive it, why do you boast as if you had not received it?'

God created each one of us with a special body, intelligence, personality and ability to work. These gifts are to be used for the benefit of all members of the church or, as Paul has written, the gifts are given by Christ, 'for the equipping of the saints for the work of ministry, for the edifying [that is, building up] of the body of Christ...' (Ephesians 4:12).

In our local church, which I'm sure is like most congregations, we have men with God-given gifts for the eldership, while others have the gifts that make them fine deacons. Other folk display skills in dealing with people, and we have one man, Keith, who welcomes people to worship each Lord's Day. He hands out the weekly newsletter, as well as Bibles and Psalm books, and always has a smile and a warm welcome for all who come. We must understand that God has given us differing skills and abilities to use for his glory. When we are all together we make up the body of Christ in that particular place. Just as a body has hundreds of parts, so also the church worldwide is made up of hundreds, even millions, of people who are different from each other. Together we make up the bride of Christ, loved by Jesus and saved by his holy life and sacrificial death on the cross in our place, as our representative.

We are called to be tolerant of those who differ from us in some way. Differences of personality, skin colour, sex, the shape of a person's nose, or how much hair we have on our heads should not cause disharmony amongst God's people. The special gifts that Christ has given to some of his people should cause no jealousy. We are different so that we can serve each other. Someone else has skills or abilities that I do not, and the gifts that neither of us possesses are to be found among other members of the body. Put all Christians together and we make a complete group. All of

us are different, but together we make up the church which worships and serves God.

Are you part of the body of Christ? If so, are you tolerant of other people? May you prove to be a true servant of Christ and a loyal friend to all who love and serve Christ.

To think about
●●●

1. Why did God give Christians different gifts?
2. What use is to be made of the gifts God has given?
3. Do you see any special gifts that God has given you? Are you using them?
4. In what way are all Christians the same?

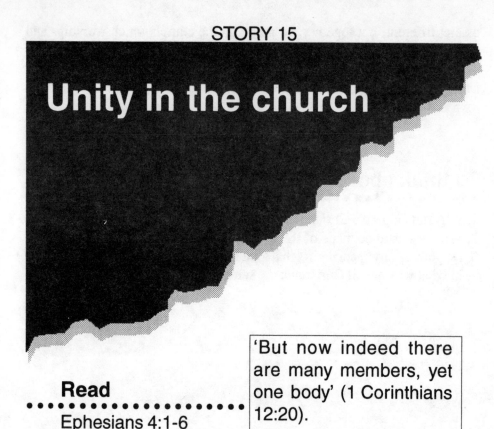

Unity in the church

Read
• • • • • • • • • • • • • • • • • • • •
Ephesians 4:1-6

'But now indeed there are many members, yet one body' (1 Corinthians 12:20).

I am amazed at the terrible happenings I read about in the newspaper and see on the TV news. Again and again I hear of families breaking up, countries torn apart by war, nations divided on political issues, and in some cases such division is accompanied by violence, killings and war.

Now the church of our Saviour, Jesus Christ, is one and the world should see us in that light but, sad to say, it sometimes becomes divided. There have been differences between Christians since the church began and these divisions have caused much heartache.

One day I was taking Wags for a walk and we came to an ants' nest. Now Wags doesn't like ants. Not long after we bought him I gave him a very juicy bone with some meat on it which he left in his favourite spot under a tree. Some time later I heard some wild barking and whimpering. When Val and I went out to see what was wrong, we found Wags looking at his bone and barking wildly. Then he began rubbing his nose with his paws. When he saw us coming he ran over and jumped up, barking and shaking his head. There on his nose I could see ants crawling about and no doubt biting his tender skin. Looking at his bone I could see that it was covered in ants. Now every time Wags sees ants on his bone he refuses to touch it. Instead he barks loudly till we come and brush them away.

ANTS WORKING
TOGETHER

Watching the ants at work we noticed that they all seemed to know what they were doing. Some small ones had actually made a narrow track which they could walk along without difficulty. If we could have seen inside the ants' nest we would no doubt have seen the queen laying eggs while all the other ants were busy carrying out their jobs in peace and harmony.

And that is how it should be in families. Mum and Dad should love one another and so provide a place of love and security for their children. But, sad to say, this is not always the case, as in our age nearly half of all marriages end in divorce.

What should be the situation as far as the church and individual Christians are concerned? There should be peace and love for the reason given in today's reading. All Christians have so much in common. It doesn't matter what our nationality, sex, age or occupation is; we all love the same Lord Jesus Christ and are saved by his death for us on the cross. We all worship the same God, who is the heavenly Father of all who believe in the Lord Jesus Christ.

The reason why we have so much in common is that we are all born again by the Holy Spirit, and the Holy Spirit who indwells me is the same Holy Spirit who indwells all of God's people. This is the baptism of the Holy Spirit which takes place in the hearts of all of Christ's people. We are all born again, have a God-given saving faith in the Lord Jesus, have been made sons and daughters of the living God and are members of the kingdom of Christ. Together we make up the spiritual body of Christ — we are the building blocks of his church, in whom God dwells by his Spirit.

All of us believe all the biblical doctrines that are essential for salvation. We are not divided over the truth that the saving work of Christ is the only way of salvation. We know that our works do not save us. We believe in one God who is three persons — Father, Son and Holy Spirit — and together we believe that Christ is God, the one who is revealed in the Old Testament as 'the LORD', Jehovah. We all have that great assurance, or confident hope, that we are saved and one day will live in Christ's presence for ever.

The church of the Lord Jesus Christ is one, and while we might have differences over baptism, what we sing in worship or the way the church is organized, these differences should not spoil our fellowship. They must not divide us, because we are one in the Lord Jesus Christ. My spiritual brothers and sisters are to be found in different churches and whenever we meet they are my dear friends. I love them in Christ. Do you?

We are all different in many ways, but together we make up the church, the bride of Christ. We are commanded to take care of each other, as the apostle Paul said: 'Let each of you look out not only for his own interests, but also for the interests of others' (Philippians 2:4).

Disputes between members of the church must be solved. Paul told two women at Philippi, Euodia and Syntyche, to live at peace with each other because their disputes had upset the peace of the congregation.

Christ gave instructions how Christians should solve their disputes (see Matthew 18:15-17). If this is followed in love, the peace of the church will be maintained.

Jesus prayed for the unity of the church. We read Christ's words where he prayed for all who would believe through the preaching of the word, 'that they all may be one, as you, Father, are in me, and I in you; that they also may be one in us...' (John 17:21).

We are to love one another and together work for the glory of God. This is one of the ways we witness to the world that we love Christ. The apostle John wrote, 'If someone says, "I love God," and hates his brother, he is a liar; for he who does not love his brother whom he has seen, how can he love God whom he has not seen? And this commandment we have from him: that he who loves God must love his brother also' (1 John 4:20-21).

All Christians are different from each other (just have a look around when you go to church next Sunday), but as we have so much in common, peace between Christians is a must — anything less is sin!

Are you working to maintain the peace and unity of your congregation? I hope that you are.

To think about

1. As we go about we see many different churches, but the Bible tells us that the church is one. What does this mean?
2. So that Christians get on well with one another we must be 'tolerant'. What does this mean?
3. Disputes often raise their heads in the churches. How should they be solved? Read and discuss Matthew 18:15-17.

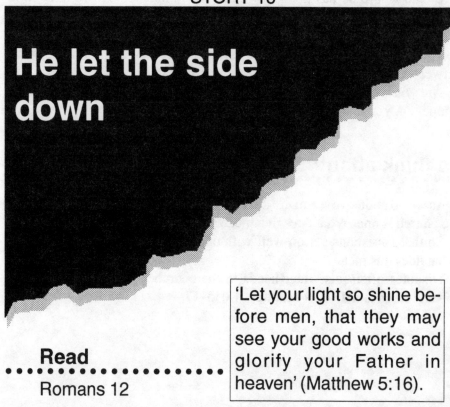

He let the side down

Read
. . . .
Romans 12

> 'Let your light so shine be-
> fore men, that they may
> see your good works and
> glorify your Father in
> heaven' (Matthew 5:16).

Some time ago I read in the newspaper of a man who claimed to be a Christian being found guilty of a serious crime. In court he admitted to the charge and was sentenced to a time in jail. His solicitor, hoping that the judge would be lenient when sentencing the man, said that his client was a Christian and was very sorry for what he had done.

When I discussed the newspaper report with a church elder his comment was: 'Yes, it's very disappointing. He certainly let the side down!' What he was saying was that the man charged with the crime should never have committed such a wicked action. What he did would have been sinful whoever did it, but for a professing Christian to be guilty of such things was especially serious since it brought shame upon the name of Christ and all Christians. I only hope and pray that the man truly repented of what he had done, for God forgives all who genuinely repent of their sins and ask his forgiveness on the grounds of Christ's death on behalf of sinners.

Christians need to be very careful when speaking about the sins of others, because we read in Scripture, 'By the grace of God I am what I am' (1 Corinthians 15:10). We must continually praise God for making us what we are and for keeping us from sinning against him. We owe God so much!

We who are called to faith in Christ must live holy and upright lives. We are not to live to please ourselves, but in such a way that Christ is glorified. By our lives we want people to recognize that we are members of God's kingdom. The apostle Paul wrote that we are saved by the grace of God through faith in Jesus Christ for a wonderful purpose: 'For we are his workmanship, created in Christ Jesus for good works, which God prepared beforehand that we should walk in them' (Ephesians 2:10).

Today's reading outlines an important aspect of the way Christians are to live, both with other Christians and with people in the society round about us. Ours is to be the life of love, shown in our kindness to others, whether they are Christians or not. Think about verses 14 and 19: 'Bless those who persecute you; bless and do not curse... Beloved, do not avenge yourselves, but rather give place to wrath...' That attitude is not usually found in the world today, as most men and women want their own way. I wonder how many parents teach their children the philosophy of the world: 'If he hits you, then hit him back!' This is to teach our children to sin! It is hard to turn the other cheek, but Christ has called us to live peaceful lives of love and concern for others. Paul wrote, 'The kingdom of God is not eating and drinking, but righteousness and peace and joy in the Holy Spirit' (Romans 14:17).

There are times when we need the protection of the law of the land against those who would harm us, but we are never to take personal revenge on someone who hurts us. We are to use the gifts that God has given us for the benefit of all people, and especially for our brothers and sisters in Christ.

What should be done to those people who profess faith in Christ, because they want to be known as Christians, yet continue to live like non-Christians because they do not belong to Christ? The answer, I believe, is to be found in a story told about Alexander the Great. Alexander was a great warrior who conquered Greece and a large part of the known world before the Roman Empire came into existence. His soldiers were known for their bravery; they were great warriors.

One day a frightened young soldier was brought before Alexander, who was told that he had deserted his companions in the heat of the battle. He was a coward! When Alexander saw the frightened young man he felt sorry for him but he had to make a decision concerning him for the sake of maintaining discipline. He could have had the deserter put to death, but instead he spoke kindly to him.

'What's your name?' Alexander asked the soldier.

'Alexander, sir,' replied the terrified deserter.

When Alexander heard the man say his name was Alexander, he thought for a moment. He didn't want any shame to be brought on the name he held so precious. He looked at the young deserter and said in a very stern voice: 'Either change your name or change your behaviour!'

So it must be with all who claim that Christ is their Lord and Saviour. We must live according to the laws of Christ's kingdom and so bring glory to Christ. If people who profess faith in Christ do not live as Christ expects them, they are to be faced with the command: 'Either change your name (i.e. stop calling yourself a Christian), or change your behaviour!'

May God's Spirit keep all of us who have trusted in Christ loyal to his commands. Pray that Satan might be kept far from us, because we know that he goes about 'like a roaring lion, seeking whom he may devour' (1 Peter 5:8). We need the all-powerful grace of God to keep Satan away, or we shall fall into sin. May God keep us faithful as we honour him in all that we do.

Of course it may be that some of my readers are not living as Christians should because you are not really Christians at all. If so, you need to realize that you cannot change your own behaviour and live a life that is pleasing to God by your own efforts. You need to go to Christ, confessing your sin and asking his forgiveness and salvation. If you do, you will then find that you are a changed person who wants to live in a way that pleases God and brings glory to him.

To think about

. . . .

1. In what way do our good works, if we are Christians, bring glory to God?
2. Who was 'Alexander the Great'?
3. What does the word 'Christian' mean?
4. How do Christians hurt the Lord Jesus and other Christians?

The loneliest man in the world

Read
• • • • • • • • • • • • • • • • • • •
Luke 23:26-49

> 'My God, my God, why have you forsaken me?' (Matthew 27:46).

No one likes loneliness. God created us for friendship with himself and with other people. However, sin completely spoiled the friendship that was meant to exist between God and his creation. Throughout the world people try to fill the gap left in their lives when man's fellowship with God was broken by inventing their own gods. Then they work out some way to worship the god they have made. In some places people have even sacrificed humans to the gods they have invented. Through such terrible sacrifices they hope to win the friendship and blessings of their god.

We live in communities where we can talk to one another, work with each other and help each other. People marry so they can have close fellowship with one particular person of the opposite sex.

Of course, there are people who like being alone, but this is not what most people want out of life. Many are lonely and hate it. There are many elderly people in our cities and towns who have outlived their friends, and sometimes even their families, and have no one to take a real interest in them at all. Others are in hospital, all alone, and may have been like that for many years.

There are very many lonely people in the world, but recently the newspaper headlines in Australia (and maybe in other countries of the world) were about someone they called 'The loneliest man in the world'. The man

was Raphael Dinelli, who was taking part in a round-the-world sailing race, in which each yacht was manned by one lone sailor. That in itself must have been a lonely life, but then unexpected events took place which proved to be terrifying for Raphael Dinelli.

In a violent storm Dinelli's yacht capsized. He was about 1,000 nautical miles from Antarctica and 1,300 nautical miles south-west of Western Australia. The temperature almost reached freezing-point and the wind was howling at sixty knots. Raphael was trapped in his upside-down yacht but was eventually forced to scramble out of it as the smell of oil made him violently ill.

There he stood, on the bottom of his upturned yacht, with waves breaking over him. As the yacht began to settle into the cold seawater he soon found himself standing up 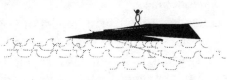 to his knees in water. What a lonely man he was standing there in the freezing cold air and water! At any moment he was in danger of being washed into the ocean. Without fresh water or any food to eat, he managed to keep his balance on his upturned yacht for a day and a half, until an Australian Air Force Orion rescue plane dropped him two life rafts containing food, water and supplies. Soon after he scrambled onto one of the life rafts his yacht sank to the bottom of the ocean. He was later rescued by another sailor who was taking part in the same yacht race.

As lonely as this man was, there was another man, the God-man Jesus Christ, who experienced a loneliness that no one else would ever suffer. He, who was God in the flesh, was nailed to a cross and suspended between heaven and earth, where crowds of people stood pointing at him and laughing. Some of the spectators mocked him, calling on him to come down from the cross. Blood dripped from the places where nails had pierced his flesh. His face was covered in blood from the cuts made by a crown of thorns that some cruel soldiers had forced upon his head. His back was coated with dried blood from such a severe whipping that he was unable to carry his cross to the place of execution.

There on the cross Christ, our Saviour, hung all alone, deserted by his friends and the disciples. They wanted nothing to do with him, fearing that the authorities would put them to death too.

But the worst part of Christ's loneliness was due to the fact that his Father had turned his face away from his Son. Jesus really was all alone on that cross. He felt the curse of God upon him because he carried the sins of his people. That is why he cried out in horror, 'My God, my God, why have you forsaken me?' (Matthew 27:46).

Satan and his demons tormented Christ through the crowds who mocked him as he died. Then the sky grew dark and this made Christ's loneliness even worse. Jesus Christ hung there on that cross, all alone, so that all who trust themselves to him might never be alone.

Christians are God's people who have been called out of the terrible darkness caused by a life of sin, which separates us from God. We live in the light of Christ and eternal life is ours. That means we shall one day enjoy perfect fellowship with God in Christ as well as perfect fellowship with all the saints.

Those who do not repent of their sins and turn to Christ, but go on living for themselves and their sins, will one day be condemned to experience the 'blackness of darkness for ever' (Matthew 22:13; Jude 13). That will be total loneliness.

Reader, go to Christ, repent of your sins and become a faithful follower of Christ. When the Lord Jesus is your Saviour you will never really be lonely again, as he will also be your Friend, and you can look forward to an eternity of wonderful fellowship with him and his people.

To think about
● ●

1. The Bible tells us that God the Father forsook his Son, the Lord Jesus Christ, when he was hanging on the cross. What does this mean?

2. Why do you think hell is called 'outer darkness'?

3. Jesus was 'forsaken' by God so that his people might never be forsaken. What does this mean?

4. If you are a Christian remember always to say 'Thank you' to the Lord Jesus for saving you.

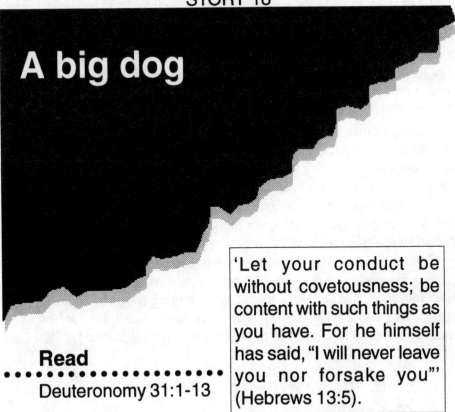

A big dog

Read
• • • • • • • • • • • • • • • • • •
Deuteronomy 31:1-13

'Let your conduct be without covetousness; be content with such things as you have. For he himself has said, "I will never leave you nor forsake you"' (Hebrews 13:5).

What a wonderful promise we read in Hebrews 13:5, where God has promised every one of his people that he will never leave them, no matter what the circumstances of their lives might be! This promise was just what the people of Israel needed to hear as they prepared to enter the promised land. The leadership of God's people was being handed over to that godly man Joshua, as the aged Moses was soon to die. The people needed courage to face the difficulties that lay before them, and that courage came from the fact that God would be with them and fight for them.

During our lives we may have many acquaintances, but most of us have very few people we can really call friends, who will stand by us at all times.

My brother John rang me recently to tell of an incident when he was prospecting for gold. He decided to go out alone in a very sparsely settled part of the bush. He had looked over his maps showing where gold had been found by prospectors in the early days of Australian settlement, and picked a

75

spot where he thought he might discover a big nugget of gold. He parked his car under a tree and had begun unpacking the gear when he heard the sound of something running towards him. Quickly he turned around to see a huge dog about twenty metres away racing towards him and frothing at the mouth. John didn't want to be attacked by the dog, but he also knew he wouldn't have time to get back into the car.

Bravely he faced the dog and said, 'Down, boy!' The dog came to a stop about fifty centimetres from where John was standing and then jumped up. He put his paws on John's shoulders and there, about thirty centimetres from his nose, a huge dog stared him straight in the eyes. The dog seemed to smile as the white froth dribbled down from his large shining teeth. Poor John wasn't sure what to do, so he quietly repeated, 'Down, boy', as he carefully helped the dog down to the ground. Then, looking at the dog's collar, he read the name 'Boss'.

Boss seemed friendly enough and all day he followed John around, only leaving his side to have a swim in a nearby dam. When John started to dig a hole looking for gold, Boss would start digging too. Maybe he thought there were rabbits in the hole! He shared a sandwich with John at lunchtime and seemed sorry to see John leave in the car when night-time fell. But John

kept a watchful eye on Boss all day as he wasn't too sure if he would remain friendly at all times.

What a wonderful promise we have as our text! If we translate the original language literally, God's promise reads like this: 'I will never, no never leave you, nor ever forsake you.'

The apostle Paul said the same thing when he wrote, 'Who shall separate us from the love of Christ? ... For I am persuaded that neither death nor life, nor angels nor principalities nor powers, nor things present nor things to come, nor height nor depth, nor any other created thing, shall be able to separate us from the love of God which is in Christ Jesus our Lord' (Romans 8:35,38-39).

God has promised — and our God can never lie — that not one of his people will be lost. God will never leave his people. No saint will perish eternally. God is always with his people in all the circumstances of their lives. He is with us in the good times and the difficult times. Our God is infinitely good, wise, faithful, powerful and unchangeable. So all of God's people can say with boldness, 'The Lord is my helper; I will not fear. What can man do to me?' (Hebrews 13:6).

Christians can face the world with boldness and true courage. We can even face that last enemy, death, with a quiet confidence, because we know the truth of David's words: 'Yea, though I walk through the valley of the shadow of death, I will fear no evil; for you are with me...' (Psalm 23:4).

The writer to the Hebrews spoke of the terrible sufferings endured by God's people because they loved and followed Christ (Hebrews 10:32-35). Ungodly men and women had attacked them, stealing their property and throwing many of them into prison. Other saints showed great courage by visiting their friends who were locked up. And why could Christians rejoice in such terrible circumstances? The writer of the epistle gave the reason: they knew that they had 'a better and an enduring possession for [themselves] in heaven' (Hebrews 10:34).

Today the situation for many Christians is no different. In some parts of the world their homes are being burned to the ground; they cannot get work; some are molested, or attacked, while others are locked up in prison. And, sad to say, many Christians are martyred even today. Why is this so? Christians love God and serve the Lord Jesus, while the world hates God and his Christ. As a result they hate all who follow Christ.

So, Christian friends, remain faithful to Christ in all circumstances, remembering that you do not face the difficult times alone because God has promised to remain by your side every moment of your life.

Joshua and the Israelites trusted God who promised to be with them when they crossed into the land of Canaan. God fulfilled his promise and as we read the book of Joshua we find that the people of Israel were victorious in their battles against the inhabitants of the promised land. This is the same God whom we love and worship. Truly we have a wonderful God.

To think about
●●●

1. The tenth commandment says that we must not 'covet'. What does that word mean?
2. Christians talk about 'the perseverance of the saints'. What does this mean?
3. Learn one text of Scripture that teaches that God will never desert his people.
4. We have a lot of possessions that we shall have to leave behind us when we die. What do Christians have which will be theirs for ever?

A foolish dog

Read

Psalm 2

'He who sits in the heavens shall laugh' (Psalm 2:4).

Both Val and I were tired and needed a break from routine, so we decided to spend a couple of weeks at the beach. We had the opportunity to stay at a holiday cottage which overlooked the Pacific Ocean. With just a short walk of twenty metres, our feet were in the sand and salt water. But what were we to do with Wags? The cousin whose house we were using said, 'Take Wags with you.' So Wags came on our holiday.

Several of our grandchildren, Aimee, Scott and Joshua, packed Wags' holiday bag with his squeaky toys, bean-bag bed and tins of food. With this and all of our gear we set off for Lennox Head, a small coastal village.

Wags obviously knew something was about to happen as he kept very close to us all the time we were packing. He was very happy to jump in the car, unaware that he faced a six-hour drive. When we stopped after about fifteen minutes to make sure the computer was with us Wags saw an Alsatian dog, about four times as tall as he is. Wags was safe in the car so he barked furiously at the dog, who just looked at little Wags and walked past as if to say, 'He wouldn't be even one mouthful!'

Later, when a huge semi-trailer pulled over beside us at some traffic lights Wags jumped to his feet and, looking up at the driver of the very large truck, started barking as if to say, 'I would like to chase you! I'm a big dog!'

Further along the highway, a police car sounded its siren and we were pulled over. Val was driving and knew she wasn't exceeding the speed limit. 'What have I done?' she asked me as she searched through her handbag for her licence.

Carefully watching the policeman walking towards us with his breath-testing gear in his hand, Wags started barking at the top of his voice. He wasn't going to have a well-armed policeman stopping his car! I had to grab Wags and hold him still and quiet while Val was breathalysed. When the policeman looked at little Wags who was snarling furiously at him, he just laughed and said, 'Call that a dog?' He thanked Val for her co-operation and sent us on our way. As we drove off, he again looked hard at Wags, who was still barking. He had a broad smile across his face.

I immediately thought of Psalm 2 and in my mind pictured silly little Wags standing before the throne of God and barking. Yet that is what Psalm 2 tells us about godless humans. Men and women think they are so powerful that God has no place in their lives. Many say that God exists only in the minds of foolish Christians and laugh at the gospel story concerning Christ. Others have the idea that if God does exist then he is not really interested in what humans do. Men and women believe they are in control of their own lives and in their minds they try to dethrone God. To so many people, God has no power. They think they can shake their fist at heaven and say to God, 'I'll do as I please and you can do nothing about it!'

However the psalmist clearly tells us that when that happens, 'He who sits in the heavens shall laugh' (v. 4). Men and women might think they can pull God off the throne of his power, but that can never be. Our God has all power, and that power and authority has been delegated to our Saviour, the Lord Jesus Christ.

Try to imagine a baby ant looking up at an elephant and saying, 'I'll kill you!' The elephant would simply burst out laughing as he carefully put his foot down on top of the ant.

In history there have been governments who have tried to kill the church by burning the Scriptures and murdering Christians. Some nations have done away with the Lord's Day. However, every effort of those wicked rulers has come to nothing, because our God rules this earth — not men and women, not Satan, but God.

When sin entered the world God's plan for the redemption of his people commenced. Satan and men and women tried to prevent the coming of Christ, but all their efforts came to nothing. Today, Christ rules this world. He is the Head of the church and the psalmist urges everyone to 'kiss the Son' (v. 12). To kiss a ruler was a sign of peace. God thus urges everyone to make peace with himself, by 'kissing' his Son.

We 'kiss the Son' when we go to Christ with genuine repentance in our hearts, seeking forgiveness. We 'kiss the Son' when we put our faith in the eternal Son of God and trust our salvation to him alone. When we make peace with God through faith in Jesus Christ, God has made peace with us. No longer does he laugh at our foolish efforts to live without him, but we see his smile of love and approval.

The psalmist concludes this psalm with some wonderful words: 'Blessed are all those who put their trust in him' (v. 12). Have you put your trust in Jesus Christ? I pray that if you have not already done so, you will do so before it is too late.

To think about
■■

1. Our text tells us that there is a time when God, in heaven, laughs. What is the cause of God's laughter?

2. We kiss people we love. What does the psalmist mean when he commands people to 'kiss the Son'?

3. There are times when people have very good reasons for rejoicing. List some of those times.

No clothes

'Blessed is he whose transgression is forgiven, whose sin is covered. Blessed is the man to whom the LORD does not impute iniquity...' (Psalm 32:1-2).

Read
• • • • • • • • • • • • • • • • • • •
Revelation 3:14-22

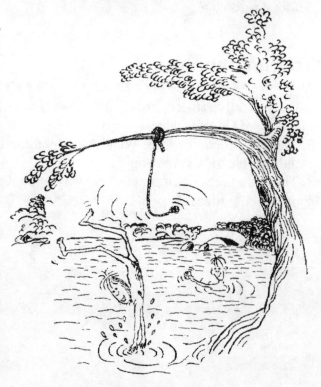

There are times in our lives when we don't wear clothes — we are naked. Every time I have a shower or a bath I undress. I'm sure that some of my readers can remember times when they went 'skinny-dipping', as we say in Australia — swimming without clothes on. John and I grew up on a farm with a river flowing along one side of our farming property. We had a great time rowing our boat about on the river where we caught a lot of fish. There were many times when we went swimming without the permission of our parents. Taking off our clothes, we would dive into the water and have a lot of fun swimming naked. After scrambling out of the water we would soon dry in the sun, put our dry clothes on and walk home.

However, all of us expect to go about each day wearing clothes. We get dressed when we get up each morning as I'm sure we would feel very embarrassed if we went to work or school without clothes on.

Not long ago, Simon and Aimee, who had been looking forward to a holiday with Nan and Pop, came to stay with us for a week. When they arrived in the car with their mum and dad they were very excited to be at long last with the grandparents who live with Wags. Then out came all the packages of toys, books, special foods and...? But where was the suitcase containing their clothes? Mum asked Dad, 'Didn't you pick up the suitcase? It was on our bed.' But the reply was: 'No, I thought you'd taken care of that.'

So Aimee and Simon had arrived with only the clothes they were wearing. When they discovered their clothes were left at home they burst into tears. They thought that to be without clothes would be a very unpleasant experience. As it turned out, they were able to borrow some clothes from their cousins and the next day they sat down to breakfast neatly dressed.

I would like to ask you a simple question: when you die and stand at the gateway that leads into heaven, what will you say if you are asked, 'Why should you be permitted to enter paradise?' I hope you know the answer to this important question because your salvation depends upon it!

God, the great Judge, is able to see us as we are — as sinners. If we stand at the gate of heaven covered in our sins we shall not be allowed to enter. We need a covering for our sins. We need to be dressed in such a way that God cannot see our sinfulness. How can this be done?

Our text speaks of sins that are covered, and the covering we need is one made out of the righteousness of Jesus Christ. In plain words, our clothes are not good enough for heaven and we need some clothing made by God himself. When Adam and Eve broke God's commands they realized they were naked. They were ashamed of their sins and their nakedness in God's presence, but God provided an answer to their difficulty: he made some clothes for them. We read in Genesis 3:21: 'Also for Adam and his wife the LORD God made tunics of skin, and clothed them.'

The parable of the prodigal son speaks of the sinful son repenting and returning to his father, when he confessed that he had sinned against God's law and against his father. When the father knew his son was truly repentant, he was asked to come inside the family home — but not straight away! He was still dressed in his dirty clothes, which were a reminder of his past sinful life. The young man's father called out to his servants and said, 'Bring out the best robe and put it on him, and put a ring on his hand and sandals on his feet' (Luke 15:22). When the son was dressed in the beautiful clothes given to him by his father, he was permitted to enter the house.

When we read about the glory of heaven, again and again we read of the saints being dressed in special clothing. In Revelation 7:9 we have the picture of all the saints standing before the throne of God and of the Lamb, and each one of them is dressed in white robes. Our reading speaks of people who were naked but did not realize that they were. The Lord Jesus urged the members of the church at Laodicea to buy 'white garments' (Revelation 3:18) so they might be clothed.

So I ask the question again: 'Why should you be permitted to pass through heaven's gates and enter paradise?' You must realize that you are a sinner who needs a covering for your sins. Our text tells us that the person whose sins are covered is blessed. We need to be clothed in righteousness, perfect righteousness, and that comes from God. We need the righteousness that comes from Christ! And, praise God, we read in Jeremiah 23:6 that Christ is called 'THE LORD OUR RIGHTEOUSNESS'.

Jesus lived a life of perfect obedience to his Father and God. He did this in our place and now, if we trust in him, his righteousness is used to cover us. We do have a covering for sin. Then we can tell heaven's gatekeeper that we have the right to enter heaven because Jesus Christ was punished in our place for our sins and we are covered in clothing made of his righteousness.

Jesus Christ has done all that is necessary for his people to enter heaven. We are clothed in his perfection. Let all who have faith in Christ give him thanks for what he has done to save us. If any of my readers do not yet know him I urge you to call upon him now, confessing your sins and trusting him to save you, so that you too may be 'clothed in his righteousness'.

To think about

• •

1. Heaven is a place where there is no sin. What does this mean, and why is there no sin in heaven?
2. Why do Christians need spiritual clothing in order to enter heaven?
3. What is the clothing Christians need, and how do they get it?

He murdered my father!

Read
Matthew 18:21-35

'Forgive us our debts, as we forgive our debtors' (Matthew 6:12).

Every day as we read our newspapers and watch our TV news broadcasts we hear of terrible crimes being committed. Today I would like to tell you about a situation that occurred in Australia in 1997. I'm sure that in every country in the world similar events have taken place.

A murderer who had killed three people was sentenced to life imprisonment, and while in prison he murdered one of the inmates. For this new crime he was sentenced to another fourteen years' imprisonment. Having completed twenty-four years in jail he asked that he be paroled, claiming that he was a changed man and had paid the penalty for his terrible crimes. He asked for a second chance. The judge who heard his appeal decided, with others, that the man should be released from prison under strict supervision.

As the murderer was being taken back to prison so that the release procedures could be sorted out he came face to face with the daughters of some of the men he had murdered. He looked at the ladies and said, 'I killed your fathers, and for that I am truly sorry... If I could give my life and bring your fathers back, I would gladly do that, but I can't. It's up to you whether you forgive or whether you hold the hatred in your heart.' Then he went on to say, 'I sincerely apologize from the bottom of my heart for what has happened...'

Now try to imagine yourself in the position of those daughters and that it was your father who was murdered by this wicked man and his friends. What would your answer be? Would it be like that of one of the women who shouted back to the man who killed her father, 'You ask me to forgive you! How could I ever forgive you! How could you ask for forgiveness? I hope you rot in hell!'? I feel sure that many of my readers would understand how this woman felt. However, if you are a Christian, what must be your reply?

When Jesus taught his disciples to pray, we find the words used in our text: 'Forgive us our debts, as we forgive our debtors.' Here Jesus was teaching his disciples and all Christians how to pray. We can only ask God to forgive us if we forgive those who have hurt us and asked us for forgiveness. This is a difficult command to obey because Jesus is plainly saying that if we are asked to forgive someone, then that is exactly what we must do.

Today's reading is about forgiveness. Peter had a problem: if someone offended him, he knew he must forgive that person and he thought he was being generous when he said that he would forgive someone seven times for the same offence. But Jesus said that Peter, and all Christians, had to go on forgiving all who asked for forgiveness, not just seven times, but 'seventy times seven' (v. 22). That means we must go on forgiving each time a person comes to us and, with sorrow in his heart for the way he has offended us, asks for our forgiveness.

We may find this very hard to do, but God demands it of us. There must be no hatred in our heart, nor must we ever hope that one day we shall be able to do something hurtful to the person. And we must never go on living with the hope that something terrible will happen to the person who hurt us.

86

In today's parable Jesus spoke of a man who was forgiven a great debt he owed to the king. Even though he himself had been forgiven he went outside and had another man thrown into prison. Why did he do this? Because this man owed him a very small debt in comparison with the one he himself had just been forgiven. When the king heard what had happened he withdrew the pardon he had offered and threw the unforgiving man into prison, where he would stay until he had paid off his debt down to the very last coin.

Jesus is teaching us that God, who is a great King, forgives the sins of his people even though those sins are terrible in his sight. Many people have had to confess their murders and other terrible crimes to God, and they have found forgiveness. They in turn must also forgive every person who has offended them and who asks them for forgiveness. Christ warns us all that if we do not forgive all who ask for forgiveness, then we cannot expect God to forgive us our sins.

'But,' you might say, 'I've been terribly hurt by what that person did to me!' Jesus tells you, 'If that person asks for forgiveness, then you must forgive from the bottom of your heart.' And Jesus demands that you mean it when you say you forgive the person. No one can truly worship God if he or she has not forgiven others. In fact Jesus commands each one of us: 'Therefore, if you bring your gift to the altar, and there remember that your brother has something against you, leave your gift there before the altar, and go your way. First be reconciled to your brother, and then come and offer your gift' (Matthew 5:23-24). Do you notice what Christ is teaching here? If you have offended your fellow Christian you must go to the person and put things right. You need to say, 'I'm sorry.' Even when someone has hurt you, you must go to that person and sort it out. You cannot say, 'I'll never speak to that person again. He hurt me and now it's up to him to come to me and apologize.' No! It is still your responsibility to go to the person who has hurt you and sort the matter out.

So the question needs to be asked: do you say the Lord's Prayer? If so, do you truly mean it when you pray, 'Forgive us our debts as we forgive our debtors'? May God give you the grace to be able to forgive all who ask you for forgiveness.

To think about
• •

1. Why did Peter tell Christ that he would forgive those who hurt him seven times?
2. Why should we forgive as many times as we are asked for forgiveness?
3. How many times does God forgive you? Why does he forgive you?
4. There are times when it is very difficult to forgive someone who has hurt us. What are we then to do?

Ouch, that stings!

Read
. . . .
1 Thessalonians 4:13-18

'The sting of death is sin, and the strength of sin is the law. But thanks be to God, who gives us the victory through our Lord Jesus Christ' (1 Corinthians 15:56-57).

There are many creatures in our world that can sting. Many years ago as I was mowing the lawn I felt a very severe pain in my shoulder. I had been mowing under a tree and couldn't believe the severity of the pain. I stopped the mower and as I made my way into the house I called out to Val, asking her to come and help me. When she looked at my shirt she saw about twelve small wasps having the time of their lives. They were stinging my flesh time and time again — and it hurt! Later I had a look at the tree where the stinging began and there I found a wasps' nest.

Bees are different from wasps as they can only sting once. Their stings have barbs on them, so once they are stuck into the flesh they stay there. The poor bee tries to get away after stinging and the back of its body

is torn away. The bee then dies. Just one sting and that's it! I remember Michael, a boy at school, who was stung by a bee. When I heard him crying out in pain, he was wildly shaking his arms about, terrified that the bee, which was still crawling up his arm, would sting him again. I was able to knock the bee to the ground and settle Michael down by telling him that the bee was almost dead. Then I got to work and pulled the sting out of his arm.

There are many things in this life which we say have a sting in them. I'm sure that many taxpayers say that tax payments have a sting to them. Often when you are sick you find out that the sickness, and sometimes the doctor's treatment, hurts — it has a sting in it!

Our text tells us that the sting of death is sin. Now we should all understand that death is not something pleasant. Humans die because they are sinners. When Adam and Eve sinned in the Garden of Eden, by breaking God's law, the death sentence came into existence. Sin brought death. Death, then, is a terrifying event to all who have not made peace with God by having their sins forgiven. Death for them is the doorway to judgement and hell has another victim.

I'm sure that every reader has visited a cemetery where many, many people have been buried. As we gaze about we might think that surely death has the victory, because these people are well and truly buried and they are seen no more. All that they owned has been divided up amongst friends and relatives mentioned in their wills. However, the truth is that death is not victorious and Paul tells us very plainly that Christ has overcome the sting of death. This is proved by the fact that three days after his death the Lord Jesus Christ rose from the grave. Death's power was broken by our Saviour.

All of you who live by faith in Christ can face death with a true hope in your heart because your sins have been forgiven and you do not have to bear the punishment of God — Christ has already been punished in your place. God's punishment is like that of the sting of a bee — it stings only once! So for all who are Christians death is not the doorway to judgement, but the doorway to heaven and joy in the presence of Jesus Christ, our God and Saviour. Christ has been 'stung' in place of all his people. When faced by death, Christians have no need to be afraid, because they know that soon they will be with Christ, which is better than anything the world can offer.

Death is not pleasant for anyone because it means that the soul and body are separated. However, there is good news for all of God's people: there will be the resurrection of the body when Christ returns. Today's reading is about the resurrection. On that day Christ's people will have glorious bodies like that of Jesus Christ himself. The apostle John has written that it has not been revealed what we shall be like on that day, except that when we see him we shall be like him (1 John 3:2). Our bodies will be perfect. There will be no more pain, no more ageing, no more weariness; no more wrinkles, a full head of hair, all our own teeth; but, best of all, we shall be perfect in righteousness.

Because of the glory that awaits us we can face death with confidence. The apostle Paul wrote of death, which he called a 'sleep', in this way: 'For if we believe that Jesus died and rose again, even so God will bring with him those who sleep in Jesus... For the Lord himself will descend from heaven with a shout, with the voice of an archangel, and with the trumpet of God. And the dead in Christ will rise first. Then we who are alive and remain shall be caught up together with them in the clouds to meet the Lord in the air. And thus we shall always be with the Lord' (1 Thessalonians 4:14-17).

Unless Christ returns beforehand you and I will face death one day. If you are a Christian, death has no sting for you because Christ your Saviour has been stung by death in your place. Dying may not be pleasant, but in your heart you will have a true joy knowing that soon you will be with Christ. You will know that the best is yet to be!

If you are not a Christian, come to Christ for forgiveness and salvation from sin and all its consequences. Then you too need fear death no more.

May God bless you all!

To think about
• •

1. Why is death such a terrible event?
2. Most people are very fearful of death. Why?
3. Dying is not a pleasant experience, even for Christians, but should Christians fear death? Why not?
4. What is the most exciting thing associated with death?

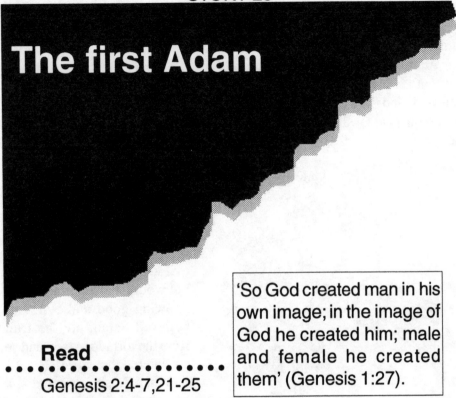

The first Adam

Read
• • • • • • • • • • • • • • • • • • • •
Genesis 2:4-7,21-25

'So God created man in his own image; in the image of God he created him; male and female he created them' (Genesis 1:27).

God created the heavens and the earth out of nothing. Then on the sixth day came the climax of creation — man! We read, 'And the LORD God formed man of the dust of the ground, and breathed into his nostrils the breath of life; and man became a living being' (Genesis 2:7).

This man was called Adam. He consisted of body and spirit and was created to serve and have fellowship with God.

Adam was created in God's image. This does not mean that because we each have a body of flesh and blood God has the same. The Bible tells us plainly that God is spirit. Adam was both flesh and spirit, which meant he could live in the world God created, while at the same time having communion with God.

Adam was created morally upright. He loved God, loved the things that pleased God and lived according to God's law. Adam was capable of making decisions, and all of his decisions should have been made in accordance with God's law.

God was the Creator and Ruler of the universe but he appointed Adam to be his ruler over the creation. Adam was placed in the land of perfection, the Garden of Eden, where everything he needed for food and comfort was to be found. God then commanded him to care for the garden as well as all the creatures. Eve was formed from Adam's rib to be his wife and at first she proved to be a perfect partner and helper for him. They were commanded to have children and so populate the world.

So there in the Garden of Eden Adam was the representative of the human race — the head, or father, of mankind.

Adam was on trial in the Garden of Eden. God had given him everything except the use of the fruit of two trees: the tree of the knowledge of good and evil and the tree of life. God warned Adam in plain language what the consequences of disobedience would be: 'You shall surely die' (Genesis 2:17).

I'm sure my readers know the story of Satan, in the form of a serpent, appearing to Eve and tempting her to sin. He said that eating the fruit of the tree of the knowledge of good and evil would not result in death, but would make her like God, knowing good and evil. Eve believed Satan, ate the fruit from the forbidden tree, and so sin entered the world.

When Adam appeared and was given the forbidden fruit to eat, it seems he did so without much thought. This raises the question: 'Why did Adam eat the forbidden fruit when he clearly knew God's command?'

I don't know the answer, but I believe that he looked at Eve, who, he knew, had already eaten the fruit, and saw that she was still alive. Maybe he thought to himself, 'God said that on the very day we ate the forbidden fruit we would die — and Eve did not die. Perhaps God didn't mean what he said, as his threats haven't been carried out. Could Satan be telling the truth?'

Whatever the reason, Adam ate the fruit and immediately his body became subject to physical death and both he and Eve began to grow old.

Also, the instant they ate the forbidden fruit, Adam and Eve died spiritually. Without the work of a Redeemer, and left to themselves, they would one day be cast into hell.

Sin corrupted Adam totally: body, soul, mind, conscience — everything! Adam was the representative of the human race. His rebellion against his Creator became our rebellion; when he sinned, his sin became our sin. And with the exception of Jesus Christ, every person born into this world inherits both Adam's sinful nature and his guilt before God.

Sin did not just partially maim or disfigure Adam and his descendants, but all were ruined totally. The human spirit is like a dead body which can no more reach out to Christ for salvation than a dead body can get up and walk. The Bible clearly teaches: 'There is none righteous, no, not one; there is none who understands; there is none who seeks after God' (Romans 3:10-11). How true it is: we are all 'dead in trespasses and sins' (Ephesians 2:1). It was King David who wrote, 'Behold I was brought forth in iniquity, and in sin my mother conceived me' (Psalm 51:5).

The first Adam, the man of the earth, is responsible for all our troubles: our pains, tears, sorrows and death. Having inherited his sinful nature, we sin and bring terrible troubles upon ourselves, including the great enemy, death. All about us we see the truth of God's words: 'For dust you are, and to dust you shall return' (Genesis 3:19). The Scriptures speak of only two men who entered heaven without passing through death — Enoch and Elijah.

If Christ does not return soon, you will one day face death, both physical and eternal — unless you know the last Adam, the Lord Jesus Christ.

To think about

1. Who was the first Adam and where did he come from?
2. In what way was Adam created in the image of God? After all, God is 'spirit' and humans are flesh and blood.
3. Why did God provide Adam with the woman named Eve?

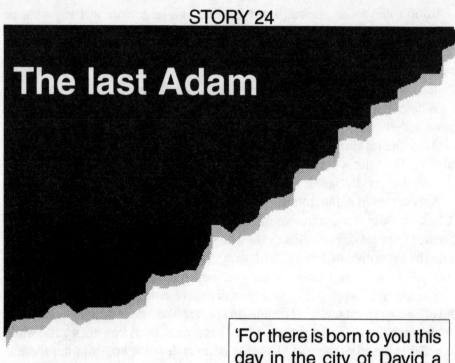

The last Adam

Read
••••••••••••••••••
1 Corinthians 15:45-49

'For there is born to you this day in the city of David a Saviour, who is Christ the Lord' (Luke 2:11).

The first Adam failed God by sinning, and so plunged the human race into despair and death.

The last Adam, the Lord Jesus Christ, came into the world to save sinners and to do what the first Adam did not do. Jesus Christ would, as the representative of his people, live a life of total obedience to God. In addition he would, on behalf of his people, bear the punishment for their sins.

The last Adam is both God and man in the one person. He is God's Son and the son of Mary. His two natures always remain unchanged; they were not mixed together to produce something totally different — he is both perfect God and perfect man in the one person.

If we think about the names given to our Saviour we learn something about him.

First he is *Lord*. This means that he is Jehovah, the Second Person of the Godhead. If we read Isaiah 6:1-3 we find the prophet Isaiah having a vision of Jehovah, seated upon a throne, surrounded by seraphim who declared: 'Holy, holy, holy is the LORD of Hosts; the whole earth is full of his glory' (v. 3). The apostle John declared that the vision seen by Isaiah was of none other than Jesus Christ (John 12:41).

Our Saviour is most truly *God*, for John wrote of him: 'In the beginning was the Word, and the Word was with God, and the Word was God' (John 1:1).

The Son of God came into this world from heaven (John 3:13; 6:62) by way of a virgin's womb — his mother Mary conceived a baby by the power of the Holy Spirit. Joseph was told by an angel concerning his beloved Mary: 'And she will bring forth a Son, and you shall call his name JESUS, for he will save his people from their sins' (Matthew 1:21). The name of this child tells us what he would do. He was called Jesus, which means 'Saviour'. Yes, he would save his people from their sins!

Many times we find Christ speaking of himself as 'the Son of Man' (e.g. Matthew 16:13). He had to be *man*, as he would be the representative of his people. The first man, Adam, had sinned and it was necessary for the last Adam to be truly man to accomplish what the first Adam failed to do.

Jesus Christ, as our substitute, had to be man. The writer to the Hebrews said, 'Inasmuch then as the children have partaken of flesh and blood, he himself likewise shared in the same, that through death he might destroy him who had the power of death, that is, the devil... Therefore, in all things he had to be made like his brethren, that he might be a merciful and faithful High Priest in things pertaining to God, to make propitiation for the sins of the people' (Hebrews 2:14,17).

As a true *man*, but one who was perfectly sinless, Jesus would suffer and die in the place of his people. Because he was *God*, the sacrifice of himself had infinite value.

Our Saviour is also called *Christ*, which means 'the Anointed One'. He was anointed with the Holy Spirit, and that without any limit.

So the last Adam is both God and man in the one person. He is true God and true man in every way.

The Saviour's entrance into this world was a great act of humiliation. Christ, the Second Person of the Godhead, the Creator of the universe, stepped down from his throne of glory; Christ the King of glory humbled himself.

Of this act the apostle Paul wrote: 'Let this mind be in you which was also in Christ Jesus, who, being in the form of God, did not consider it robbery to be equal with God, but made himself of no reputation, taking the form of a bondservant, and coming in the likeness of men. And being found in appearance as a man, he humbled himself and became obedient to the point of death, even the death of the cross' (Philippians 2:5-8).

As Jesus walked the streets of Jerusalem, with dust on his body, perspiration on his face, tired and hungry, he went unrecognized as God, the Creator of all things. He lived a life of perfect obedience to his Father, as our representative, doing what the first Adam should have done. Then, just as

Adam's sinful nature and guilt were passed on to all of his descendants, so Christ's perfect obedience is imputed, or credited, to all of his people.

When Christ died on the cross he did so as the representative and substitute of his people, willingly accepting the punishment of God that was due to his people for their sins. Christ became our sin-bearer!

His sacrifice for sins was accepted by God as all that was due to his sinful people and God put Christ's righteousness to their account.

The last Adam saved his people perfectly. Now each one of them is forgiven and has the righteousness needed to enter heaven.

Christ's saving work also meant the giving of the Holy Spirit, who works the miracle of regeneration (that is, the new birth) in the hearts of all whom the Father gave to his Son (John 14:16-18; 17:6-9). As a consequence the power of sin in their lives is broken and they are brought to repent of their sins and made able to serve and worship God.

The last Adam also won for his people glorified bodies, because the day will come when Christ returns and all the dead will rise from their graves. The godless will rise to shame and everlasting contempt, while God's people will rise with glorified bodies, like that of the Lord Jesus Christ.

These new bodies will be controlled by the Holy Spirit, because our souls will be made perfect in righteousness. Thus we read the wonderful words of the apostle Paul concerning the last Adam: 'And so it is written, "The first man Adam became a living being." The last Adam became a life-giving spirit... The first man was of the earth, made of dust; the second Man is the Lord from heaven. As was the man of dust, so also are those who are made of dust; and as is the heavenly Man, so also are those who are heavenly. And as we have borne the image of the man of dust, we shall also bear the image of the heavenly Man' (1 Corinthians 15:45,47-49).

Let us thank God for the provision of the last Adam, for salvation is found in him alone.

To think about
•••

1. Why is Jesus Christ called the 'last Adam'?
2. Learn a text of Scripture that teaches us that Jesus Christ is Jehovah.
3. Jesus was called 'the Son of God' and the 'Son of Man'. Why were those names used?

Shipwreck!

Read
••••••••••••••••••••
1 Timothy 1:12-20

'Therefore we must give the more earnest heed to the things we have heard, lest we drift away' (Hebrews 2:1).

Every year many ships are wrecked and end up on the bottom of the ocean, which means the loss of valuable ships, all the cargo and often the loss of lives.

There are many places in the world where safe harbours are protected by great rocky headlands. When a ship enters the harbour there is safety, even if a storm is raging and the seas are huge. However, one problem often experienced by sailors is getting the ship into the harbour during rough seas. During bad weather we often see many ships out at sea, riding out the waves, until it is safe to make their way through the harbour entrance.

Long ago when sailing ships sailed the world the difficulty of entering the harbour was far greater than it is today because they depended upon the wind to move about, and shipwrecks were even more common. So in times of storm, most of the ship's sails would be furled, while the sailors waited for calmer seas in order to enter the safety of the harbour. However, there are many headlands where ships were wrecked. Unable to sail through the gap between the headlands into the safety of the harbours, they were blown closer and closer to the rocks where they were smashed to pieces. It is dangerous for ships to drift about on the ocean without any power. They need to be continually under the control of the sailors who steer them to a safe harbour.

There are many 'drifters' in this world — people who have no home of their own. They drift about from place to place and many end up as human wrecks. Today's text and reading are both about people who drift in spiritual matters. They never seem to come to an understanding of the truth. They have their Bibles, but are led astray by the winds of spiritual doctrine invented by foolish people. For a time they seem settled and happy in a congregation, but soon they move off to another group, and then off to yet another. These people are the spiritual 'drifters'. Paul warned the Ephesians that they must not become spiritual 'drifters' who would be 'tossed to and fro and carried about with every wind of doctrine, by the trickery of men, in the cunning craftiness of deceitful plotting...' (Ephesians 4:14).

The writer to the Hebrews warns his readers that they must take care not to become 'drifters' who miss the 'harbour'. There were many Jewish people who loved Christ in those early days soon after his resurrection. They loved Christ and with God's help became obedient people. However, when persecution broke out many were forced to leave their homes and possessions and escape to some place of safety. Others began to question the teachings of Christ and the apostles and turned back to their old way of life. They began 'drifting' in their spiritual life, so the writer to the Hebrews warned all 'drifters': 'Beware of drifting because you might miss the harbour where there is safety.' The place of safety is Christ and fellowship with his people. Of course, perfect safety will be ours when we are with him in the kingdom he has prepared for all of his people.

Our reading mentions two men, Alexander and Hymenaeus, who were heretics. They had become spiritual 'shipwrecks' when they rejected the gospel preached by Paul. They were no doubt encouraging other people to become spiritual drifters as well. Together they would miss the 'harbour' of the Christian faith. Their destiny would be hell unless they found repentance.

Later on we read a severe warning to the Hebrews: 'If we sin wilfully after we have received the knowledge of the truth, there no longer remains a sacrifice for sins, but a certain fearful expectation of judgement... It is a fearful thing to fall into the hands of the living God' (Hebrews 10:26-31).

When people leave the congregation of believers and turn their back upon Christ, where can they go for safety? Christ is the only way of salvation. No one else has paid the penalty for sin; so these 'drifters' can search high and low, but they will never find safety in any other beliefs or way of life.

The parable of the sower (Matthew 13:1-9,18-23) speaks of people who once said they loved Christ but when the going became difficult returned to the world. There they became spiritual 'drifters' on their way to hell. They missed the safety of the harbour and made shipwreck of their souls.

There is a warning here to each one of us: remain faithful to Christ regardless of what happens. Keep with the people of Christ and don't become a spiritual 'drifter'. If you remain faithful to Christ you will one day enter the heavenly harbour.

May you be one of those people who will live eternally with Christ.

To think about

1. What do you think causes people who claim to be Christians to 'drift' away from Christ?
2. How do we know our pastor is teaching us the truth?
3. Why should we spend time reading the Scriptures and praying?

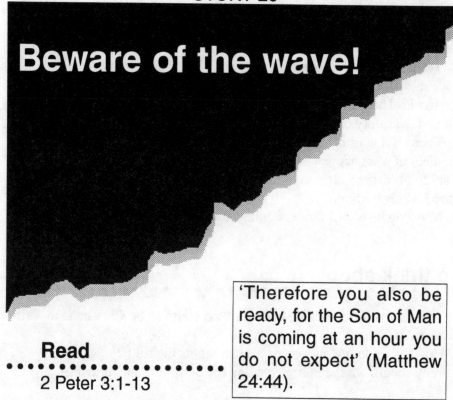

Beware of the wave!

Read
• •
2 Peter 3:1-13

'Therefore you also be ready, for the Son of Man is coming at an hour you do not expect' (Matthew 24:44).

Jesus Christ is going to return to this world of ours one day and this is good news for Christians. Our Redeemer is coming to take us to the heavenly home he has prepared for us. However, the question that is asked again and again in the Bible is: 'Are you prepared for that day?' We know that Christ will return, yet the Bible warns us that many believers will be caught unawares. They know that Christ is returning, but are not ready day by day for the great event.

Part of the problem is, as Peter tells us, that it has been a long time since the announcement was made that Christ would come again. However, we must be ready for his return and not be found unprepared when he comes.

Some years ago Valerie and I had a holiday in Tasmania, the small Australian state that is separated from the mainland by Bass Strait. To get across Bass Strait we had the choice of an aeroplane or a boat. We chose the boat as we wanted to take our car with us so we could do a lot of sightseeing. We visited many lovely places, but before long it was time to board the ship and sail back to the mainland. When the ship was leaving the harbour we stood on the deck and, with the cool air blowing on our faces, watched the places of interest along the shore. As the ship moved along quite a large wave spread out from the bow and made its way towards the shore, which was not too far away.

On the shore we saw a fisherman who had taken his boat to a ramp where it could be floated onto his trailer and taken home. I suppose he had caught plenty of fish because we sailed near enough to see that he was smiling and looking pleased as we sailed past. So there he and his friend stood, one hanging onto their boat, the other leaning on the trailer which was attached to the station wagon. The rear door of the car was open and it was obvious

that they had been packing some of their fishing gear safely away in the back. They stood beside their boat and watched our ship slowly moving down the river towards the open sea. We waved, as did hundreds of other passengers, and they waved back. They were so interested in the ship and in waving to the passengers on deck that they were unaware of the wave being stirred up by the passing ship. Too late they saw what was happening. Suddenly the wave picked up their boat and dumped it down about thirty metres away from the loading ramp. The wave then washed completely over their trailer and poured in through the open rear door of their station wagon. I feel sure from what I saw that their car was flooded with water. The two men, for a moment or two, were standing in water up to their necks. Then as we sailed out to sea the poor fellows just looked around in amazement at what had happened.

They must have known that a large ship would make a good-sized wave — but they were not prepared for what was sure to happen. I can well imagine that it took some time and help from others in order to get their boat onto the trailer. Then there would be the problems caused by the gallons of salt water which flooded their car. No doubt they would eventually have arrived home with a sorry tale to tell their wives, explaining their late arrival.

The message from this story is that we must be ready at all times for whatever may happen. If you are a member of the Scouts or Guides you will know your motto: 'Be prepared!' As a Christian your motto concerning the return of Christ is the same: 'Be prepared!' Jesus put it very plainly when he said, 'Watch therefore, for you know neither the day nor the hour in which the Son of Man is coming' (Matthew 25:13). You and I must be ready at all times because Jesus said in our text that his return would be at an hour when he was not expected. Everyone will be going about their activities on that day, just as they would have been the day before Christ returned. We shall all be concerned with earning a living, making sure the house is tidy, getting ready for examinations at school and all the other things that take up our time and thoughts, when suddenly the heavens will part like a piece of paper torn in half and Christ will appear with all his glorious and most powerful angels. The angels will gather all his people together from all places on earth, even from the cemeteries, and then we shall always be with our Saviour.

Are you ready for that day? Our reading in 2 Peter tells us what to do in preparation for Christ's return: live a godly life! Are you living a life that pleases Christ? Remember that Jesus said that we are to show our love to him by keeping his commandments.

Of course, only those who have repented of their sins and come to Christ for salvation can live a life that pleases him. If you have not yet put your trust in Christ as your Saviour and Lord you need first to come to him for salvation. Otherwise the day of his coming will be a truly dreadful day for you, because it will mean you have left it too late and you will face the awful prospect of God's judgement of condemnation — eternal hell.

May we all be prepared for that wonderful day when he returns. May the day not catch us unprepared!

To think about
●●

1. What does the Bible tell us about the date of Christ's return to earth?
2. How are you and I to prepare for his return?
3. How are we to show our love of the Lord Jesus?

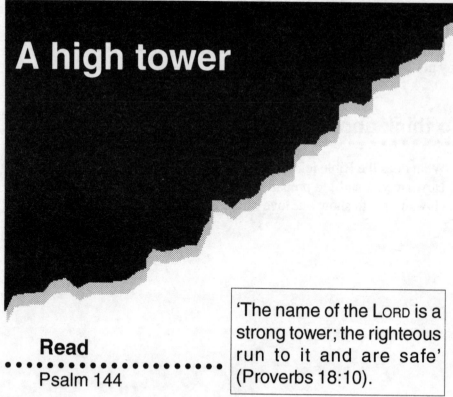

A high tower

Read
Psalm 144

> 'The name of the LORD is a strong tower; the righteous run to it and are safe' (Proverbs 18:10).

Some time ago I received the story below from a friend who is pastor of a congregation in one of Australia's capital cities. He comes from Ireland and this was his story.

Many Australians have come from other countries and I happen to be one of those people. I was born in Ireland and I grew up there. Now there have been people living and building houses in Ireland for many years. In fact, in the same year we were celebrating the two-hundredth anniversary of European settlement in Australia, Dublin, the capital of the Republic of Ireland, was celebrating its two-thousandth anniversary.

This means that there are some very old buildings in Ireland and I want to tell you about some of these buildings called 'high towers' or 'round towers'. There are a number of these, or their ruins, scattered about Ireland. They are tall, high, round towers, built very strongly, rather like lighthouses, but without lights. There is, however, one peculiar thing about them — if you walk around the bottom, looking for the way in, you won't find one! There is no door at the bottom! Instead the door is high up on the side!

Can you imagine why anyone would want a tower like that? It would be very difficult to get into, wouldn't it? And that is exactly why they were built that way!

106

You see, there were Christians living in Ireland nearly sixteen hundred years ago and those towers were built by some of them. They were built near old abbeys, where Christians were living together. In those days, they were always likely to be attacked by Viking pirates coming in boats across the sea. Those pirates would kill everyone in the abbey and steal anything that was worth stealing.

The Christians couldn't fight the Vikings — very few people could — but they thought of a plan to keep themselves and their property safe. They built these high towers and, when the alarm was given that the Vikings had landed, a place of safety was waiting for them.

We can only try to imagine the organized confusion when the signal came for the people to escape. I'm sure everyone knew exactly what to grab and take to the tower. The precious manuscripts would be the first to be placed in the tower. Maybe the people had a supply of food there, ready for the day when it would be needed. They would carry all their valuables up a long ladder and into the tower through the doorway half up the side. Then, when the last person was safe inside, the ladder would be carefully pulled up and in through the doorway. With the door tightly closed the people would just sit there in safety until the Vikings went away! The Vikings couldn't get to the door, for, even if they had a ladder, the people in the tower could just push it down again!

I don't know for certain where the Christians got the idea for building these towers, but I sometimes wonder whether they got it from the Bible. You see, the Bible speaks in a number of places about 'high towers', and it often says that God is like a 'high tower' to his people. The people who come to him are kept safe from the attacks of the devil.

There is a Judgement Day approaching when every person will stand before the Judge of the universe, the Lord Jesus, to be judged according to the perfect standard of God's law. All are sinners, so where will our protection be on that day? The Judge will be the protector of his people! Of course, to find protection you must have gone to Christ, confessing your sins and putting yourself under his protective care. You must be trusting Jesus Christ alone for your salvation.

In the Book of Psalms we find the writer saying that God is 'my fortress, my high tower and my deliverer; my shield and the one in whom I take refuge' (Psalm 144:2). And then there is a verse in Proverbs which sounds just like those Irish Christians many years ago running to their high tower when they heard that the Vikings were coming: 'The name of the LORD is a strong tower; the righteous run to it and are safe' (Proverbs 18:10). Learn this text and its place in the Bible. However, of greater importance is this: have you done what the text says? Have you run to God and found safety? In other words, have you turned your back on your sins and put your trust in the Lord Jesus to save you?

To think about
● ●

1. We read that the LORD is a 'high tower'. What does this mean?
2. The Bible tells us that we need protection; but what do we need protection from?
3. How does God protect his people from his own anger?

Lest we forget!

Read
••••••••••••••••••
Luke 22:14-23

'For as often as you eat this bread and drink this cup, you proclaim the Lord's death till he comes' (1 Corinthians 11:26).

Today, as I sit in front of my computer, it is 25 April. Now to most people throughout the world this date is not very important, but to people in Australia and New Zealand it is a public holiday. It is ANZAC Day! It is a special day set aside for the people of both nations to remember the sacrifices of men and women during wartime. It is our 'Remembrance Day'! The word ANZAC stands for Australian and New Zealand Army Corps and tells of a time during the First World War when a force of mainly Australian and New Zealand soldiers landed on the shores of Gallipoli to fight against the Turks. Thousands

of soldiers died in the months following the landing and for our men and women it ended in defeat.

And so today in both countries men and women who fought in all wars are having remembrance services and marching to remind the nations

of the great sacrifices made during wartime. We remember those young men and women who fought and died in the hope that their friends and relatives back home might live in freedom and peace. We owe those men and women a great debt. As the wreaths are laid the crowds who gather around will say, 'Lest we forget!' We must never forget those brave people who fought to give us freedom and a safe, peaceful land in which to live. We owe them all so much.

Now all who are Christians are commanded to remember a great event that took place two thousand years ago — the death of the Lord Jesus Christ. We are commanded to remember the one who died that all the citizens of his kingdom might live in peace with God and be able to worship him as they should.

When you look at our text and reading for today I hope you understand how we are to remember the saving sacrifice of the Lord Jesus. He has commanded his people to sit together and eat bread and drink wine — the ordinary food of Christ's day — in remembrance of his death. The bread speaks to us of his body that was broken as it was whipped and nailed to the cross. The wine speaks to us of that precious blood that was shed on that awesome day. Bearing our sins, Christ was punished by God in the place of his people. This simple communion service is called the Lord's Supper. At the Lord's Supper we sit down to eat and fellowship with like-minded friends, as well as with the one who has invited us to sit at his table. We eat the bread and drink the wine together to remember the Lord's death — and this is the way God commanded us to remember Christ's death, until he comes again.

When I sit at the Lord's table, I look about me and see my Christian friends, my brothers and sisters, with whom I will spend eternity. How we should love our Saviour who gave himself that we all might live for ever with him!

I know I owe a great debt of gratitude to all those men and women who fought and helped in many ways to ensure I live in freedom. Because of them I have freedom to speak, freedom to move about my country, freedom to think the thoughts I want to think, freedom to read all the good books I want to read, freedom to vote for the men and women I want to have in government — but, most important of all, I have freedom to worship God as he has commanded me to do. All of these freedoms are so important. However, Christ, through his death on the cross, has also given me freedom! He has broken the power of sin in my life and I am now free to love and serve him. Sin does not rule in the lives of his people. The Lord's Supper should always remind us of the great debt of gratitude we owe our Saviour.

There is a day set aside for us to remember something special about the Lord Jesus Christ, and that day is Sunday, the Lord's Day. On the first day of the week Jesus Christ broke free from death and rose again. So we gather with God's people each Lord's Day for a time of worship. Sunday is the day when we remember that Christ was victorious over death. One day you and I will die, unless Jesus Christ returns beforehand, but if we are Christians death will have no power over us. When Christ returns again he will raise our bodies from their resting-places and then we shall be with the Lord for ever.

Never let us forget the debt we owe our Saviour. His death seemed to be a defeat, but it turned out to be victory for all of Christ's people. Through his death we are saved and have become citizens of heaven. We owe our Saviour so much. Lest we forget!

To think about
●●

1. Each year the Jews celebrated their leaving the land of Egypt with Moses as their leader. What was that celebration called and what was done?
2. What special way do Christians remember the sacrificial death of the Lord Jesus?
3. The bread and wine used in the remembrance meal remind us of something special. Of what are we reminded?
4. What is there in the life of the Christian that reminds us of the resurrection of the Lord Jesus?

Branding

Read
••••••••••••••••••••••
Matthew 12:31-37

'By this all will know that you are my disciples, if you have love for one another' (John 13:35).

Branding hurts! When we lived on the farm it was necessary for Dad to brand our cattle. Every now and again he would attend the cattle sales to buy some new milking cows. When they were unloaded at our farm the new cows would have their brands checked. All the farmers had their own registered brands which were burnt into the skin of the animals. The scar

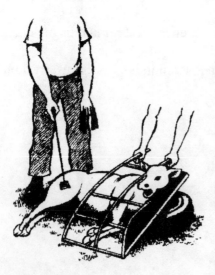

made by the brand was always clearly visible to everyone, as never again would hair grow on that part of the skin. So Dad was obliged to put his mark on the cattle he bought.

The cows were rounded up into a small yard while John and I made a fire. Then we would put the steel branding iron into the red-hot coals and there it would remain till it was glowing as red as the coals around it. With the cow held firmly in place Dad would quickly grab the handle of the branding iron and burn the brand mark into the skin of the poor animal, which would usually give a

bellow of pain. After some antiseptic had been splashed on the burn the cow was allowed to go free. A week or so later the brand mark could be clearly seen. Thinking back to those days, what we did was very cruel to the poor, dumb animals. Now animals are marked in different ways, which are not as painful as using a red-hot brand — they have a tag fixed in their ear or on their tail. However, the brand was a clear mark indicating who owned the animal.

There are many ways in which we are marked to indicate that we belong to one group or another. At secondary school I wore a black-and-white school tie. That was the special mark of boys who attended Maitland Boys' High School. Everyone wore ties and badges that marked us out as a special group. Playing football meant we wore our black-and-white jerseys which showed that we were 'magpies' — named after the black-and-white birds found in many countries. That was the mark indicating who we were. As you walk down the street, have a look at the many different badges worn by people. Those badges are 'brands' telling us something about the people who wear them.

One day as I was reading the Bible I had a sudden thought of what would make a good brand mark to be used on people who professed to be Christians. I was reading the tenth chapter of the Gospel of John when I came to verse 27: 'My sheep hear my voice, and I know them, and they follow me.' I stopped and thought about the words, and for some reason I thought of branding cattle. And there I could see the brand the Lord might use to mark his people out as belonging to him. Christ's people 'hear' and 'follow' him. So the brand used by Christ could be one depicting an ear and a foot. Yes, we must all be people who listen to what Christ is saying in his Word and then we must obey his commands. We must follow in his footsteps.

But as we cannot be branded with a red-hot iron, what is it that marks us out as followers of Christ? The answer is given in our text: 'By this all will know that you are my disciples, if you have love for one another.' Christian love is the true mark of a Christian. This is the love spoken about in 1 Corinthians 13 — a love that does not boast and seeks the best for the other person, even if that person is not very likeable. Christian love does not gossip about others and tell the world about another person's failings; instead it hides the sins of other people and seeks to bring them to repentance, to be truly sorry for what they have done. Christian love is the love shown by the Good Samaritan who helped a person who hated him, and this type of love is found amongst Christians. It is easy to show love for people who are pleasant and easy to get on with, but Christian love is seen in the help and friendship given to people who are unpleasant, even those who are the enemies of Christians.

Our reading speaks of people being known by the way they live, the fruit they bear. Ungodly people do not show true Christian love. When they show kindness to others, often it is in order to be repaid in some way or another. Many people do wonderful acts of kindness, but they want their name to appear in the newspaper or on TV so that everyone will speak well of them.

Christians do not seek to be rewarded for what they do. They do their kind acts simply because they love Christ. We don't need a red-hot brand to put a mark on our bodies in order to show that we belong to Christ because all we have to do is show Christian love. That will then mark us out as being Christ's disciples.

Someone once said, 'If you were arrested and charged with being a Christian, would there be enough evidence to convict you?' The evidence should be seen in the life we live. If we are Christians, we should all be displaying the fruit of the Spirit in our daily lives: 'The fruit of the Spirit is love, joy, peace, longsuffering, kindness, goodness, faithfulness, gentleness, self-control' (Galatians 5:22-23).

If you have put your trust in the Lord Jesus and know him as your Saviour, pray daily that you will display the brand of the Holy Spirit that marks you out as being one of his sheep — true Christian love.

To think about
● ●

1. What is the 'fruit of the Spirit'?
2. What marks a person out as being a Christian?
3. We read and talk about 'Christian love'. In what way is Christian love different to the love that exists in a family? Should Christian love exist in all families?

A big fall

Read
• • • • • • • • • • • • • • • • • •
Matthew 26:30-35

I'm sure there is a little bit of pride in each one of us. There are some people who will claim, 'Well that's not me. There's not an ounce of pride in my body.' The problem is that they are proud of not being proud!

I remember reading of a minister who was told by one of his congregation that the sermon he preached was really great. His reply was: 'Yes, I know. The devil told me just as I was pronouncing the benediction.'

The Bible contains the story of the great King Nebuchadnezzar, a man who was tremendously proud of all he had accomplished. He was a great warrior king, whose armies had conquered much of the known world. He was also responsible for improving the city of Babylon, which was famous for one of the seven wonders of the ancient world, the Hanging Gardens of Babylon.

One day as Nebuchadnezzar was strolling about his royal palace and looking over his city he said, 'Is not this great Babylon, that I have built for a royal dwelling by my mighty power and for the honour of my majesty?' (Daniel 4:30).

Yes, Nebuchadnezzar was indeed a proud man. He wanted all the credit for what he had done. The true God, the God of Israel, had no part in his thoughts. In a moment of time God judged the king for his pride and he began to wander about in the fields eating grass as if he were an animal. The

115

Scriptures tell us, 'He was driven from men and ate grass like oxen; his body was wet with the dew of heaven till his hair had grown like eagles' feathers and his nails like birds' claws' (Daniel 4:33). What a fall — from being a proud, wealthy, powerful king to thinking he was an ox, eating grass. Pride certainly goes before a fall!

And this is what our text is talking about. It is a warning to all proud people who boast of their ability to do great things that these things can all disappear in a moment. I remember a great ski jumper who had made the jump many times with great success. Then there came the jump where the athlete slipped, fell over and was injured. That skier had probably thought all would be well as she had made that jump many times before — she may well have been confident that there would be no mistake — and yet she fell.

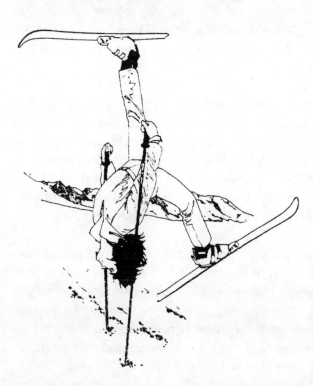

There is a warning for all Christians in our Scripture passages today: beware, because when you think you are safe and secure you could fall into sin and bring shame on yourself, other Christians and the Lord you profess to love and serve.

'But,' you may reply, 'that wouldn't happen to me. I love Christ. I read my Bible. I won't fall into dreadful sin!' That answer sounds very much like the words spoken by Peter, that brave, outspoken disciple who loved Christ and had left his work as a fisherman to follow him. Peter could not believe Jesus when he said he would die at the hands of wicked men. Then when Christ went on to say that the disciples would all desert him and be scattered, Peter proudly declared, 'Even if all are made to stumble because of you, I will never be made to stumble' (Matthew 26:33). Peter was sure that he would remain loyal, even if all the other disciples deserted Christ.

Now try to imagine how Peter must have felt when Christ told him in reply, 'Assuredly, I say to you that this night, before the rooster crows, you will deny me three times' (Matthew 26:34).

Strong, confident Peter thought he could stand firm against the might of the Roman armies and the Jewish religious leaders, yet Christ's prophecy was fulfilled. Everything happened just as he had said. When Peter was confronted by a young woman who accused him of being one of Christ's followers, he denied it — even using an oath to confirm his denial. Then the cock, or rooster, crowed just as Christ had told him it would. Peter, who was so proud of his ability to follow Christ faithfully, fell into terrible sin.

Earlier, when asked by Christ who he and the other disciples believed Jesus was, Peter had replied, 'You are the Christ, the Son of the living God' (Matthew 16:16) and had been commended for doing so. Yet it was not long after those magnificent words were spoken that Peter had argued with Christ when he had announced that he was to go up to Jerusalem and be crucified. Christ had then rebuked him sternly, calling him Satan, because he was acting as the devil's mouthpiece in trying to stop Jesus from going to the cross. Even after that Peter had not learned the truth of today's text: 'Let him who thinks he stands take heed lest he fall.'

Our reading is a warning to each one of us that we shall all suffer temptations from Satan and his demons. Let none of us think that we shall never fall into sin, because we all can and do fall, sometimes committing terrible sins. However, God has made us a promise that when we are tempted he will provide a way of escape. We shall never be tempted beyond what we can bear. Of course these great words are true for all Christians, but so often we fail because we do not use the way of escape that God has provided. We must all walk close to Christ, praying, reading his Word and mixing with other Christians who encourage us and help us live the Christian life.

May we never become puffed up with pride in ourselves or our own achievements! There is only one way the proud person can go, and that is down! Always remember that it is by the grace of God that you are what you are. If you are a Christian, you did not make yourself one; God did. After you become a Christian, you do not keep yourself faithful, God's Holy Spirit does. You owe everything to Christ.

To think about
• •

1. What is 'pride'?
2. Satan's sin was pride. He boasted about what he wanted to achieve. What did he claim? (Read Isaiah 14:12-14 and take notice of his words, 'I will...')
3. Why should none of us be proud of anything about us?
4. Peter had a big fall and the same can happen to all proud people. Let us always give all the glory to God and his beloved Son, the Lord Jesus Christ. How can you do this?

The diet is working

Read
• • • • • • • • • • • • • • • • • • • •
Romans 8:26-30

I'm on a diet! It's not my first diet. I think it must be my one hundred and first effort at losing some weight! As I read the papers and see the advertisements on TV I realize there are many people trying to diet. We see attractive, slim people who are held up before us as examples of what we should be like. As a result many people try to lose weight in the hope of becoming slimmer and better-looking.

Some months ago several people at church commented, 'You're getting chubby about the cheeks, Jim. You're looking very well.' Of course I knew what they were saying in a kind way — they really meant, 'Dear, oh dear! Jim, you're putting on weight!' Then I discovered that I couldn't do up the collar of my shirt and had to buy a larger size. When Val said, 'Jim, you'd feel much better if you lost some weight. I'm sure you wouldn't have so much back pain if you lost a couple of kilograms,' I knew I had to do some serious dieting.

119

So I had a look in my cupboard and there I saw my four special silk shirts that I hadn't been able to wear for ten years. So I made up my mind I had to lose weight. I had done it many times before and this time I meant not only to lose weight, but to keep the weight off. I would be slim and look healthy.

I have been dieting now for about four months and have lost almost 20 kilograms. I am still not able to wear my silk shirts, but within a couple of months I hope I will be. Several people have commented on how well I look and the fact that I'm almost 'thin Jim'. One lady said to me, 'Jim, you look really well. How do you feel?' All I could say to her in reply was: 'I feel hungry!'

However, Val believes I look better and thinks I should now give up the diet and maintain my weight at its present level. But I have a goal: I want to be thin like a man I know — not too thin, but just the right size — and I want to wear my silk shirts again. (I'm not giving any of my large clothes away as I may need them again next year!)

Our text and reading tell us what we should be like — we should have a character like that of the Lord Jesus Christ. We should be Christlike in all our ways. We are all sinners, but Christians know they are being changed. The old sinful ways are being put aside like the chocolate that I enjoyed eating but was bad for me. Now we are living according to the law of God. We are being sanctified by the gracious work of the Holy Spirit. God is making us more like Christ.

Just as I have a goal in my dieting, so does the Holy Spirit have a goal in his work of sanctification, and that goal is making us like Christ! Becoming Christlike is a real battle, just as overcoming the desire to eat too much is a battle. The apostle Paul wrote, 'For the good that I will to do, I do not do; but the evil I will not to do, that I practise' (Romans 7:19). Paul knew that he had a battle on his hands living the Christian life and I'm certain that all Christians have a similar battle. We want to be like Christ, but Satan wants us to sin, so he does all he can to tempt Christians to disobey the commands of their Lord. Just as many dieters fall into the trap of overeating and spoiling their diet, so also Christians fall into sin. But God is working to make us like Christ. We were not saved to be made happy, but to be made righteous — and that should make us happy! This great truth is summed up in Paul's words: 'For whom he foreknew, he also predestined to be conformed to the image of his Son, that he might be the firstborn among many brethren' (Romans 8:29).

All our lives we shall struggle to become more like Christ. This is something we cannot do by ourselves. We need some powerful help, and that help is there in the person of the Holy Spirit. Each one of us must pray that God's Spirit will make us faithful to the Christ we love and who loves us dearly.

Val knows that she will never have a perfect husband, but I keep telling her that one day I will be perfect. She laughs when I say that, but she knows what I mean — the day is coming when I will meet Jesus Christ, my Saviour, face to face. That will be a glorious day for all Christians, for then something wonderful will take place. The apostle John tells us, 'Beloved, now we are children of God; and it has not yet been revealed what we shall be, but we know that when he is revealed, *we shall be like him,* for we shall see him as he is' (1 John 3:2). There, in the presence of Christ our Redeemer, we shall stand perfect, clothed in his righteousness. When I am clothed in my perfect resurrected body I will have realized perfection.

When Moses came down from Mount Sinai his face glowed; it reflected the glory of God that had shone upon him. Christians do not just reflect the perfection of the Lord, but Christ lives in us by his Spirit.

What a great day it will be when I have reached my earthly goal and can wear my silk shirts! Following my diet has been hard work. Val has been able to eat the chocolates while I eat my piece of carrot. However, despite the difficulties, if I persevere I expect one day to reach my goal.

But what a wondrous day it will be when I am finally transformed into the likeness of Christ my Saviour. The way may be difficult (James 1:2-4) but by God's grace all his people will make it. This should be the most important goal in the life of all who declare that they love Jesus Christ.

To think about

1. Big changes are taking place in the lives of Christians. What is God's plan for everyone who trusts in the Lord Jesus?
2. Who is working in our hearts to bring about God's changes?
3. The Bible uses the word 'sanctification'. What does this word mean?
4. When will Christians be perfect in every way?

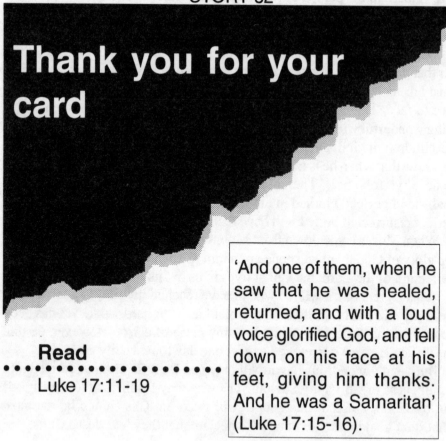

Thank you for your card

Read
• • • • • • • • • • • • • • • • • • •
Luke 17:11-19

'And one of them, when he saw that he was healed, returned, and with a loud voice glorified God, and fell down on his face at his feet, giving him thanks. And he was a Samaritan' (Luke 17:15-16).

All readers who reach the last page of my books will find a special message. I deliberately put the message on the last page so that it would only be read by people who read all the chapters. To my surprise twenty or thirty people have responded, most of them from the United Kingdom. It is always great to find a letter or card from overseas in our mail from someone who has read one of my books and I have answered all of them.

The reason I included the message was not because I wanted people to thank me for my books, but because I wanted to find out where the books ended up and to try to discover if people were finding them helpful. Nevertheless, it has been very encouraging to me to find that everyone who has replied has said 'Thank you' for the book.

It is good to hear someone say 'Thank you' and I trust you are one of those people who say 'Thank you' to everyone who helps you.

I'm sure we all owe thanks to a lot of people for their kindness. Our parents have helped us when we were growing up and many people have given of their time, energy and resources to make our life much easier. Have we thanked those people for all their help?

The Lord Jesus had performed a great miracle by healing ten lepers. Now leprosy was a dreaded disease. Lepers were not welcome in the houses and cities because people feared that they might catch the complaint. Lepers were believed to be unclean and were pushed out of society. They could not attend worship in the temple or synagogues and they were not allowed to sit down and have a meal with healthy family members or friends. They truly were outcasts. When Jesus entered the village where the ten lepers lived they would not come near him but stood a way off and called out to him, 'Jesus, Master, have mercy on us!'

I'm sure they had heard about Jesus and the wonderful healing miracles which he had performed. They must have believed that this was their one chance of being made well, if only they could catch the attention of the great healer.

Jesus heard their cries and told the ten of them to go and show themselves to the priests. The priests had to examine them to make sure they were healed. Then, and only then, would they be allowed to return to their place in the life of their village. As they walked towards the priest's house they realized they were cleansed from the dreaded disease of leprosy.

The only one of the ten who praised God for his healing was a Samaritan. He was one of those people who were hated by the Jews, but he knew that he owed Christ his life. So, praising God, he returned to Jesus and, bowing down before him said, 'Thank you for healing me.' The other nine healed lepers just went on their way to show themselves to the priests. They were Jewish people and as such should have been the first to praise God for what had happened to them. They should have led the way back to Christ to give thanks, but they did not. Jesus praised the Samaritan for coming back, for glorifying God and for thanking him for what he had done.

My little dog Wags knows how to say thanks. After eating his daily treat he comes over to me and looks up into my face as if to say, 'I love you. Thank you for being so kind.' Then as I put my hand down to pat him he turns his face to my hand and licks my fingers. I'm sure this is his way of saying, 'Thank you for your kindness.' Often he comes into my study, nuzzles his wet nose against my leg and then lies down at my feet and goes to sleep.

I feel sure that my readers can do better than Wags in saying 'Thank you'. None of us should be like those nine lepers who were healed, but did not have the time or the decency to say 'Thank you' to Christ for his miraculous healing. Each day we have so much for which to thank God.

I have food on my table (and even the fact that I have a table is something to be thankful for). I sleep in a comfortable, warm bed. I have a warm shower each day; the water is laid on; the electricity works. I drive a car. My house has a roof that keeps the rain out. My wife takes good care of me. I have plenty of books to work with. No one has invaded my home, and the country in which I live is peaceful. For all of these blessings I must continually thank my God, for it is he who has given me all these things.

However, of greater value than all of those material blessings is my knowledge of Jesus Christ as my Lord and Saviour. God saved me. He gave me a saving faith in Christ Jesus. So I must always thank him for his goodness to me and the many Christians whom I know and respect.

All who are Christians should agree with the words we find in Psalm 92:1-2:

It is good to give thanks to the LORD,
And to sing praises to your name, O Most High;
To declare your loving-kindness in the morning,
And your faithfulness every night.

Make a list of the many people who have helped you during the last few weeks and as you thank them for their kindness to you, cross off their names. But more than everything else, if you are a Christian thank God for your salvation in Christ Jesus. If you do not yet know him as your Saviour call upon him for the forgiveness of your sins. Then go on to serve him faithfully, showing him by the way you live your love and thankfulness for all he has done for you.

124

To think about

1. Make a list of the things for which you must thank God.
2. Have you ever thanked your pastor for his work in your congregation? If not, make the effort to say 'Thank you' for his kindness — and don't forget to thank his wife as I'm sure she does a lot of work in the congregation too.
3. What is the most wonderful thing that God has done for you?

My daddy's in heaven

'For I consider that the sufferings of this present time are not worthy to be compared with the glory which shall be revealed in us' (Romans 8:18).

Read
•••••••••••••••••••
2 Corinthians 11:16-33

The Christian life is not a bed of roses; there are many thorns along the way. In Australia and most parts of the Western world, Christians are tolerated, even if they are not always liked, and there is no organized persecution of the church. However, in other parts of the world tens of thousands of Christians are murdered each year, just because they love Christ and speak to others about the wonderful Saviour they serve.

When Jesus sent the disciples to preach in the cities of Israel he warned them of what lay before them: 'And you will be hated by all for my name's sake. But he who endures to the end will be saved' (Matthew 10:22). This has been the situation faced by all of Christ's followers. There are great blessings and rewards promised to all who serve Christ faithfully, despite the cruel opposition of Satan and the world. He said, 'Blessed are those who are persecuted for righteousness' sake, for theirs is the kingdom of heaven. Blessed are you when they revile and persecute you, and say all kinds of evil against you falsely for my sake. Rejoice and be exceedingly glad, for great is your reward in heaven...' (Matthew 5:10-12). So all Christians face the opposition of the world in some degree and some of them will become martyrs for Christ — they will be prepared to be put to death rather than deny their Saviour. The writer to the Hebrews spoke of the hardships that Christians endure, but he went on to say that his readers had not resisted the wickedness in the world to the point of having their blood shed (Hebrews 12:4).

In our reading we have a brief outline of the way the apostle Paul suffered as he travelled the world, preaching and serving Christ. Paul had been thrown into prison, whipped, stoned and on three occasions had been shipwrecked (read 2 Corinthians 11:23-27). During his many travels he had been hungry, without a bed, in danger of attack from those who hated him and continually criticized by the Jews and others. Yet by God's grace he remained faithful to Christ.

When we read our history books we find many stories of Christians who lost their lives because of their love for Christ. Recently I read the story of two women from Scotland, Margaret Wilson and Margaret M'Lauchlan[1], who gave their lives for Christ. They knew that Christ was the head of the church and not the king, who claimed authority over the church. These two ladies were tied to stakes on the shore of the Solway Firth in May 1685 and drowned by the incoming tide. The sentence passed on them was that they should be tied to palisades fixed in the sand, within the area covered by the water at high tide, 'and there to stand till the flood overflowed them and drowned them'. Margaret M'Lauchlan was an elderly lady, while her friend Margaret Wilson was just eighteen. Both those godly women died by drowning, tied to posts in the water, for refusing to acknowledge the king as head

of the church. God gave them courage during their trials and sent his angels to take their souls to be with Christ in heaven. Was it worth it? Paul said that it is worth suffering the worst that the world can do to us, because glory is waiting for Christ's followers. Nothing is worth comparing to the glory that awaits God's people.

Ed McCully, one of the five missionaries murdered by the Auca Indians, with his wife Marilou and son Steve, pictured at the mission station which was their base. *Photograph reproduced by kind permission of Elisabeth Elliot.*

If it is possible try to obtain a copy of *Through Gates of Splendour* by Elisabeth Elliot. It tells the story of five young missionaries who were murdered by the Auca Indians in South America in 1956. While the families were sad at hearing the news that their husbands and fathers had been murdered they knew that it was all worthwhile. Taking the gospel to the Aucas was part of their obedience to the commands of Christ, who told his people to tell the world of the salvation that was freely available in him.

Later the McCully family returned to the United States of America for the birth of a baby. When the baby was brought home little three-year-old Steve McCully, whose father was one of the murdered missionaries, looked at the crying baby and said gently, 'Never you mind; when we get to heaven I'll show you which one is *our* daddy.'[2]

Think of the great sacrifice that was made by the men who willingly gave their lives in the service of Christ and the great loss suffered by the families of those murdered missionaries. Was it all worthwhile? Read again today's text: 'For I consider that the sufferings of this present time are not worthy to be compared with the glory which shall be revealed in us.'

Yes, all the sufferings for Christ are worthwhile! When we arrive in heaven we will live in the land of sinlessness, the land of glory. There will then be no pain, no suffering, no tears and no more death, just everlasting joy in the presence of Christ, who loved us and died for us so that we might live with him.

1. This is the version of her name adopted in *The Ladies of the Covenant* by the Rev. James Anderson (Blackie & Son, Glasgow, 1853) and in *Notable Women of the Covenant* by W. Chapman (W. Sonnenschein & Co., London, 1883). Other sources give her surname as Lauchlison, MacLachan, or Lachlane.
2. E. Elliot, *Through Gates of Splendour*, Hodder and Stoughton, London, 1957, p.188.

To think about
●●●

1. Now for a hard question: where is heaven?
2. Being a Christian is sometimes very difficult. What makes following Christ truly worthwhile?
3. Why do so many people hate Christians?

Hale-Bopp visits the earth

Read
• • • • • • • • • • • • • • • • • • •
Revelation 19

'He who testifies to these things says, "Surely I am coming quickly." Amen. Even so, come, Lord Jesus!' (Revelation 22:20).

Tonight I stood outside in the cool air and gazed up into the heavens looking for something very special that should have been easily seen. Some years ago I did the same when Halley's Comet visited the earth. I can remember that night very clearly as it was the night I was ordained to the ministry and

took up my appointment as minister of a congregation. I had read a lot about Halley's Comet and could remember my dad telling me that he had seen it many years before. Halley's Comet only visits the earth every seventy-five years. However, I was very disappointed with what I saw in the sky. It was just a faint piece of light and appeared to be no better than a puff of smoke. I wasn't very impressed and after gazing into the sky for a couple of minutes decided that I would go to bed. I had been waiting for Halley's Comet for a long time and thought it was not worth the wait.

However, now as I write this another comet is visiting the earth — the Hale-Bopp Comet. I have seen a photo in the paper and it looks so colourful. I also read that the comet is one thousand times brighter than Halley's. So I have been standing outside, looking upwards, but so far have not seen anything except the stars shining brightly. Maybe tomorrow night I will find the comet — if the sky is clear and the night is dark, and I can find the right spot in the sky. The newspaper reported that the next ten nights are going to be spectacular. So, we in Australia wait and hope that we will be able to say, 'Ah!!!!' and 'Oh!!!!' when we see the brilliant

display in the heavens. Maybe we shall not see much, but we hope that we shall see something worthwhile. The world has been told when to look and where to look and most people will see if they can spot it. Maybe some of my readers will have seen it. Yes, and several days after writing the above I did see Hale-Bopp in all its glory!

In the Bible we are told of another visitor to our planet — the Lord Jesus Christ! He has appeared once as the promised Messiah and on that visit was crucified, saving his people from their sins. The world did not want Christ. However, we are plainly told that next time Jesus Christ visits our planet he will come, not as a baby, but as the King of kings, in all his power and might, accompanied by his mighty angels as well as the souls of all of his people who passed into his presence through death. The Bible warns us to be prepared for his coming and has given some clues of events that will be taking place just before he comes. We are told to look upwards, for the day of our redemption is drawing closer.

When Christ returns every person upon earth will see him. The apostle John wrote, 'Behold, he is coming with clouds, and every eye will see him, even they who pierced him' (Revelation 1:7). On that day everyone will have a perfect view of what is taking place; even those who are dead will rise again — God's people to be with Christ, and those who have not loved and served him during their lives to be banished for ever from the presence of the Lord.

The heavens will be rolled up when Christ comes, and all that blue sky will disappear. We shall see the mighty angels going about their work, guiding the saints into the presence of Christ where they will find protection from God's anger. The Second Coming of the Lord Jesus Christ will be no secret coming. Everyone will be going about, doing what they usually do: 'For as in the days before the flood, they were eating and drinking, marrying and giving in marriage, until the day that Noah entered the ark ... so also will the coming of the Son of Man be. Then two men will be in the field: one will be taken and the other left. Two women will be grinding at the mill: one will be taken and the other left' (Matthew 24:38-41).

So do not be led astray by some who teach that the Lord will come in a secret way and remove his people from the earth so that no one sees him come and go. When Christ returns he will be more visible than the Hale-Bopp comet, for everyone will see him as he descends to earth from heaven. We have been warned to be ready for that day. Are you ready? The only preparation that pleases God is going to Christ and asking him to forgive your sins and to save you. It is only when he sends his Spirit into your heart and gives you the gift of faith that you will be truly ready for that wonderful day when he returns.

You then will not be amongst those people who, when they see Christ descending in power and glory, cry out to the mountains and rocks, 'Fall on us and hide us from the face of him who sits on the throne and from the wrath of the Lamb! For the great day of his wrath has come, and who is able to stand?' (Revelation 6:16-17).

Let us make sure we are ready as the day of Christ's return is getting near! May we all look upwards and long for the appearance of the Son of God.

To think about
● ●

1. The Bible tells us that every person who has ever lived will see the return of the Lord Jesus. How can that be?
2. When Jesus came to this earth the first time he did so as a baby. Very few people knew that he had been born. Find out something about the Second Coming of Christ.
3. Why will unconverted people be terrified when Christ returns? Are you able to say you are looking forward to the return of the Lord Jesus?

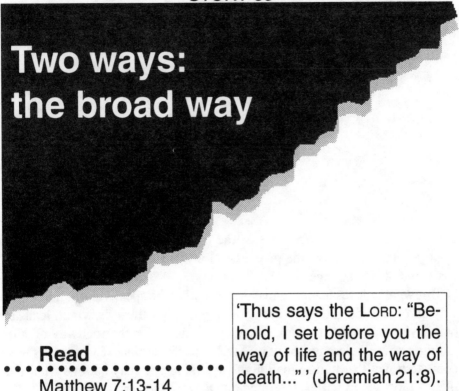

Two ways:
the broad way

Read
• • • • • • • • • • • • • • • • • •
Matthew 7:13-14

'Thus says the LORD: "Behold, I set before you the way of life and the way of death..." ' (Jeremiah 21:8).

All roads usually lead somewhere, although at times it is hard to understand why certain roads are built. One local government authority built a road which ended at the edge of a river. The money for the project had run out and there was nothing left for the building of a bridge across the river. So there the road ended, at the edge of the river, and it stayed like that for many years.

Jesus warned his hearers that before them were two gates which opened the way to two roads: 'Enter by the narrow gate; for wide is the gate and broad is the way that leads to destruction, and there are many who go in by it. Because narrow is the gate and difficult is the way which leads to life, and there are few who find it' (Matthew 7:13-14). Those two roads both lead to definite destinations and every person is called upon to make a choice as to the way he or she will travel through life.

First let us look at the 'broad way'. We must try to imagine that we are standing in a courtyard which has a clearly seen, wide gateway opening on to a broad roadway. Crowds of people are pushing their way towards the gate, each carrying a lot of baggage, and it is obvious from the smiles and laughter that this band of happy people are looking forward to the journey that lies before them. People are pointing to places that can be seen along the roadside and that look wonderful from a distance, but no one seems

133

concerned to find out what lies at the end of the road. There is no real trouble entering through the gate, even for those carrying the biggest suitcases and other baggage.

But what is Jesus teaching his listeners when he speaks about that broad way and the wide gateway? He is talking about a lifestyle which leads to hell. Everyone wants to walk that way, because it is the roadway of self-indulgence and tolerance, built by Satan and his demons. Everyone is welcome to travel that multi-laned highway where you may believe what you like — most views will be tolerated and permissiveness is encouraged.

Getting onto the roadway is very easy. Each traveller is able to carry his sins with him and enjoy them to the full. Many smiling faces are travelling the lane of sexual immorality, while others are hurrying along the lane named pride. Changing lanes is permitted and it is obvious to all that the various lanes tend to appeal to travellers according to the age-group to which they belong.

The broad way is not fenced and the travellers are encouraged to taste the delicacies of sin found in abundance beside the road. On one side of the roadway is a sign saying, 'If it feels good, do it!' Only a few people ever bother to look closely at the sign and if they do they will notice that it has been painted over a few indistinct sentences. A closer look, however, reveals: 'The way of the wicked is an abomination to the LORD...' (Proverbs 15:9). The few who see these words point, laugh and continue on their way.

No one takes any notice of a prophet who warns the travellers on that broad way: 'Do not love the world or the things in the world. If anyone loves the world, the love of the Father is not in him. For all that is in the world — the lust of the flesh, the lust of the eyes, and the pride of life — is not of the Father but is of the world. And the world is passing away...' (1 John 2:15-17). A close look reveals the skeletons of other prophets who in days past also warned the travellers of their danger. It is common knowledge that they were killed for upsetting the travellers with their warnings.

134

Another sign proudly proclaims the name 'Freedom Way', but a closer look shows that the reverse side has written on it: 'Jesus said, "Most assuredly, I say to you, whoever commits sin is a slave of sin" ' (John 8:34). But no one bothers to look back as the bright lights along the roadway are too inviting for people to turn back.

And so the crowds of people skip along, failing to notice that they are skipping and dancing on a bridge that crosses a deep ravine. It is a very deep ravine, in fact so deep that the bottom cannot be seen. Sometimes when the question is asked, 'Are we really going the right way?' the answer comes back, 'Of course we are. Look at the crowds of people. We can't all be wrong. This is the way of happiness and the end of the road will satisfy your greatest longings.' And with those words of assurance the seemingly happy throng move on.

However, there is some uneasiness amongst travellers, for many of them are at times concerned about the stories they hear. Sometimes they think all is not well on the broad way. Some 'nice' people are concerned about reports of 'adultery, fornication, uncleanness, licentiousness, idolatry, sorcery, hatred, contentions, jealousies, outbursts of wrath, selfish ambitions, dissensions, heresies, envy, murders, drunkenness, revelries' (Galatians 5:19-21) and so on, among their fellow-travellers. But most people believe that as long as they are not touched personally by such activities, all is well. The broad way is certainly a pleasant way to many. But the end of the broad way is hell!

Are you travelling along the broad way?

To think about
●●

1. The Bible speaks of the broad way and the narrow way. Why is the 'broad way' given that particular name?
2. How do people get onto the broad way?
3. Where does the 'broad way' lead?
4. There are a lot of 'nice' people on the 'broad way'. What does this mean?

Two ways:
the narrow way

> 'I have set before you life and death, blessing and cursing; therefore choose life, that both you and your descendants may live...' (Deuteronomy 30:19).

Read
• • • • • • • • • • • • • • • • • • •
Deuteronomy 30:15-20

In the previous chapter we imagined we were standing in a courtyard with two gateways. The wide gateway is easily seen by everyone, but there is another, narrow, gateway which is not clearly visible. In fact Jesus said of this narrow gate that searching is needed to find it and that 'There are few who find it' (Matthew 7:14).

There are some amongst the crowds in the courtyard who seem to be looking for that gateway. They look very concerned and anxious. John Bunyan described these people as being weighed down by a great burden of sin. More than anything else they want to be rid of their sins — something which they know is only possible if they find their way through the narrow gate. They are searching for this gateway because the Holy Spirit has revealed to them that they are sinners who need the Saviour.

The gateway is difficult to find because Satan has done all he can to hide it from view. Near the entrance to the narrow way is Good Works Forest where many travellers have spent a lifetime wandering, searching in vain for the way to heaven. But the gateway is always found by those who belong to Christ and who come to him in faith with a genuine desire to leave their old selfish ways and follow him.

When the gateway is discovered they find the way through to be very narrow and those who pass through cannot take their unconverted friends

Christian at the wicket-gate (the entrance to the narrow way)
From an old edition of Bunyan's *Pilgrim's Progress*

with them. They must leave many friends and family members behind because these people would rather travel the broad way. Pride, self-righteousness and everything that offends God and is contrary to his laws must be left outside the gateway — there is no room for baggage when passing through that narrow gate.

Looking through the gate, those who find it see a long narrow road weaving its way upwards between well-built fences. The road has only one lane and is bounded by kerb-stones.

Above the gate a name is clearly written in very large letters — 'Jesus'. Easily seen through the opening is a finger board which has on it the words: 'The Way'. Below those words are written: 'Jesus said ..."I am the way, the truth, and the life. No one comes to the Father except through me"' (John 14:6). The pathway is bounded by fences called 'God's revealed will'.

A closer look reveals a glorious city in the distance, the New Jerusalem, which is the destination of all who walk along 'the Way'. Some boldly step through the gateway while others do so quietly, but all have their eyes fixed on the destination. They know that King Jesus has prepared that way for his people to walk.

All who travel that narrow way are happy to remain on the roadway even though the bordering fences impose certain limits on their freedom of belief and action. But these regulations are the delight of the travellers, for they love the one who gave them the law, and their great desire is to be like him. They discuss the new freedom they have because the slavery to sin in their lives has been broken. No longer are they slaves of Satan and their old sinful nature. Now they find themselves free to obey the King's law and worship God. They all find true freedom in serving King Jesus. Had he not said to them all, 'Therefore if the Son makes you free, you shall be free indeed'? (John 8:36).

The narrow way is the way of living in fellowship with God, through faith in Christ, and obeying his commands. This has never proved to be a popular way to the world; only those whose hearts have been changed by God and who now love King Jesus long for holiness. They know that without holiness they can never complete their journey and enter the heavenly city.

Along the narrow way there is an abundance of fruit trees.

These trees produce the 'fruit of the Spirit' and all travellers are able to eat their fill. There is only one fruit to be picked, but each piece of fruit has stamped on the skin: 'love, joy, peace, longsuffering, kindness, goodness, faithfulness, gentleness, self-control' (Galatians 5:22-23). Each traveller is greatly refreshed by eating the freely available fruit.

Walking the narrow way often means being on the receiving end of slander, persecution and the hatred of the world. Many times the broad way is found to run close to the narrow way and where that happens many of those who travel the broad way insult and sometimes even kill the King's servants.

But God's people have their attention centred upon King Jesus and the city at the end of the road. Their fellowship with the King is the source of all their joy and they know his words of encouragement: 'Blessed are you when they revile and persecute you, and say all kinds of evil against you falsely for my sake. Rejoice and be exceedingly glad, for great is your reward in heaven, for so they persecuted the prophets who were before you' (Matthew 5:11-12).

Yes, the way can be difficult! Paul wrote of the difficulties faced by all who travel the narrow way, for he had experienced many of those hardships: 'We are hard pressed on every side, yet not crushed; we are perplexed, but not in despair; persecuted, but not forsaken; struck down, but not destroyed' (2 Corinthians 4:8-9).

God's people long to be with King Jesus in the land of righteousness, where there are no more tears or death because there is no more sin. These travellers say 'Amen' to the words of the great apostle Paul: 'For I consider that the sufferings of this present time are not worthy to be compared with the glory which shall be revealed in us' (Romans 8:18).

But how disappointing it is to see that there are only few who travel the narrow way!

To think about

1. How do you get to travel along the 'narrow way'?
2. If you have never read *Pilgrim's Progress* by John Bunyan, get a copy of the book and read it. I can still remember my mum reading it to my brother and to me each night when we were young.
3. Talk about good Christian books and make every effort to get the family reading — the Bible first and then good literature.
4. Where does the 'narrow way' lead to?
5. What can you use as your 'road map' while you travel the 'narrow way'?

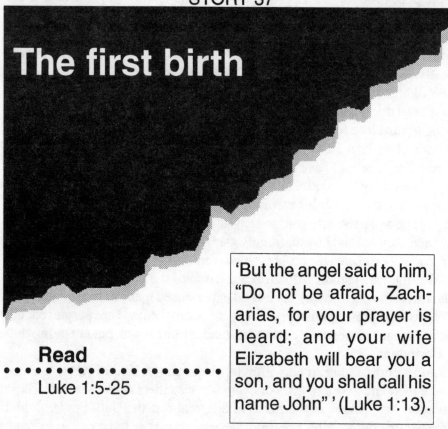

The first birth

Read
• • • • • • • • • • • • • • • • • •
Luke 1:5-25

'But the angel said to him, "Do not be afraid, Zacharias, for your prayer is heard; and your wife Elizabeth will bear you a son, and you shall call his name John" ' (Luke 1:13).

The birth of a baby is usually a time of great joy in any family. Mum and Dad bring home a small 'bundle of joy' which they proudly show off to all their relatives and friends and anyone else who is willing to have a look. When visitors arrive they point out how much the little one resembles Mum and Dad. And that's how it should be — babies all show some resemblance to their parents.

Some years ago I witnessed a very sad event. I saw a man whom I knew quite well carrying a small white coffin containing the body of a tiny baby who had lived only one day. Tears were falling from his eyes as he placed the coffin beside an open grave. The joy of that family had turned to sorrow.

Such tragedies make us ask the question: 'Why do such sad things

140

happen?' The answer is hard for humans to accept, but the Bible gives us the true explanation. Babies are born into this world with a sinful nature. We read this truth in Psalm 51:5 where David writes, 'Behold, I was brought forth in iniquity, and in sin my mother conceived me.'

With the exception of the Lord Jesus Christ, every child born into this world is like our ancestor Adam — all inherit his sinful nature. Our first birth brings us into this world having a sinful nature, which is a tragedy!

In the Garden of Eden, Adam, who was the representative of the human race, sinned and his sin ruined us all. Because we are sinners we die, as the wages of sin is death. Adam was warned that to eat the fruit from the tree of the knowledge of good and evil would mean death. Because of Adam's sin the apostle Paul wrote: 'In Adam all die...' (1 Corinthians 15:22).

This means that babies are born into this world as members of Satan's kingdom. They are sinners who need the gracious work of the Holy Spirit in their hearts — they must be born again!

With very few exceptions, all people can hear the call of Christ to repentance, when they are old enough to understand the meaning of words, because they have ears and a brain. However, as they are spiritually dead what they hear means very little to them. Something must happen to make it possible for them to believe. Ears and a brain are not enough: they need to be given a new, spiritual life, with spiritual ears to hear the truth that God has revealed in his Word, together with the ability to understand and respond to it.

The first birth puts people in a world where their lives are centred on material possessions and earthly pleasures. The attitude of most people is to enjoy life to the full because all that lies before them, apart from this life, is physical death and the grave, which they think means the end of existence.

Those who are only born once may experience many things in the course of their lives which bring them great happiness, but one day everything that matters to them will come to an end. And the end for those who are only born once is eternal death — hell. No one goes out of existence when he or she dies. The body returns to the dust, but the soul lives on to face Christ when the great judgement takes place. On that day the soul of a person who has only been born once will be reunited with the resurrected body and the whole person cast into the lake of fire to receive the fitting punishment for a whole life spent in rebellion against God and his laws.

The first birth means life, but life ruined by sin. It means citizenship of the kingdom of Satan and finally, if there is no second birth, eternal damnation. It would have been better for people who only ever experience the first birth never to have been born at all!

To think about

1. The Bible speaks of two people who were not born. Who were they?
2. Why do we need to be born again?
3. Who was the only person who has ever lived who did not need a second birth? Why not?
4. Why would it have been better for some people if they had never been born?

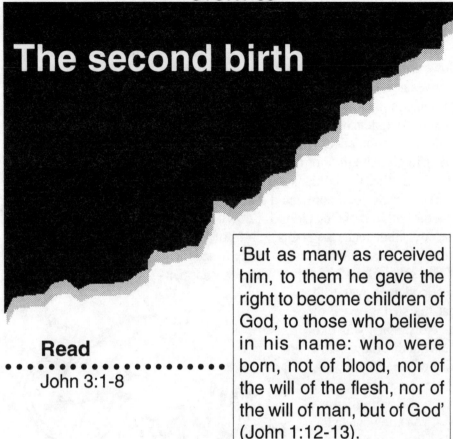

The second birth

Read
● ● ● ● ● ● ● ● ● ● ● ● ● ● ● ● ● ● ●
John 3:1-8

'But as many as received him, to them he gave the right to become children of God, to those who believe in his name: who were born, not of blood, nor of the will of the flesh, nor of the will of man, but of God' (John 1:12-13).

A man named Nicodemus visited Christ secretly one night as he wanted to find out if Jesus really was the Christ whom God had promised to send to Israel. Nicodemus was a very well-respected man in his nation, as he was a leader of the Pharisees, involved in teaching people great truths about God.

When he came face to face with Jesus he said, 'Rabbi, we know that you are a teacher come from God; for no one can do these signs that you do unless God is with him' (John 3:2).

Christ's reply totally confused Nicodemus for he was told, 'Most assuredly, I say to you, unless one is born again, he cannot see the kingdom of God' (John 3:3).

Nicodemus was to learn from Christ that not every Jew would gain entrance into heaven. The Scripture plainly taught: 'That which is born of the flesh is flesh' (John 3:6). But, as Paul wrote, 'Those who are in the flesh cannot please God' (Romans 8:8).

The first birth means we are by nature citizens of the kingdom of Satan. To gain citizenship in the kingdom of God we must be born into that kingdom — we must be born a second time.

This second birth is a spiritual birth and is entirely the work of the sovereign God, whose Spirit comes and takes away what is called 'the heart of stone' and replaces it with a 'heart of flesh' (Ezekiel 11:19).

Today many people think we live in an age when miracles do not occur. However, that is not so! The regenerating work of the Holy Spirit, in which he gives new life to those who are dead in their sins, is an amazing miracle. It is the almighty power of God, who spoke the word causing the creation to burst into existence, that changes the human heart. Paul wrote, 'For it is the God who commanded light to shine out of darkness, who has shone in our hearts to give the light of the knowledge of the glory of God in the face of Jesus Christ' (2 Corinthians 4:6).

The apostle John confirmed that it was by the second birth that people become children of God (John 1:12-13). He says very clearly that just being born does not make a person a child of God, nor does birth into a godly family. Mothers and fathers may long to see their children become children of God, but unless God acts it will never happen — we are all dead in sin!

Nicodemus was told that the saving work of the Holy Spirit was like the wind that blows. You cannot see the wind, where it comes from or where it is going. However, you know when the wind is blowing as the clouds move across the sky, the leaves on the tree rustle and you can feel the wind on your face.

God's Holy Spirit enters the sinner's heart, changes the heart and moves on to touch another sinner's heart. You cannot see the Holy Spirit, but you can tell that the new birth has taken place.

The sinner who has been born again (or, to use the correct theological term, is regenerate) has a God-given faith in Jesus Christ and, having been given a new heart, now loves God and other Christians. He (or she) now hates the sins which he once loved. He now loves God's law and by God's grace seeks to live a life of obedience to that law. The new Christian knows that he can never earn his own salvation by trying to keep God's laws, but he understands that the way to show his love for God is by obedience. After all, didn't Jesus say, 'If you love me, keep my commandments'? (John 14:15).

The new birth means that our bodies are the temples of God's Holy Spirit (1 Corinthians 6:19). His presence breaks the power sin once had in our lives, and instead of being Satan's slaves we become willing servants of the Lord Jesus Christ. In fact the apostle Paul tells us, 'If anyone is in Christ, he is a new creation; old things have passed away; behold, all things have become new' (2 Corinthians 5:17). As children of God we become citizens of heaven.

If you are a Christian then praise God for what he has done in your life. If you do not yet know Christ as your Lord and Saviour then pray that God's Spirit might convict you of your sins and give you saving faith in the Lord Jesus Christ, the only one who can save you from your sins.

To think about

1. What is meant by the 'new birth'?
2. Who brings about the 'new birth'? Are humans able to help the Holy Spirit in this great work?
3. How do we know if a person is 'born again'?

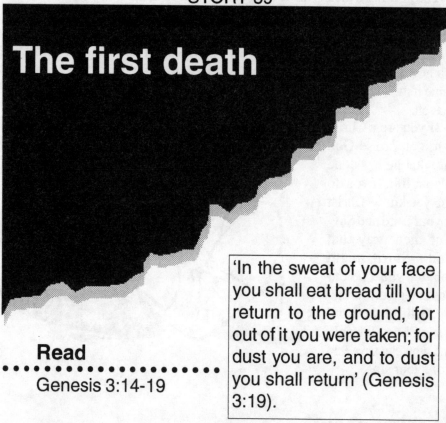

The first death

Read
• • • • • • • • • • • • • • • • • • •
Genesis 3:14-19

'In the sweat of your face you shall eat bread till you return to the ground, for out of it you were taken; for dust you are, and to dust you shall return' (Genesis 3:19).

My dad used to tell me quite often that there are only two certainties in life — death and taxes. I know he was correct concerning taxes, but I also know that one day the Lord Jesus Christ will come again and those who love him will be transformed and pass into his presence without dying.

Death is all around us and many of the folk I once knew and loved are no longer here on earth. They have died. When I visit hospitals I see people who are facing death. On the radio each morning I hear the names of those who are to be buried during the next couple of days. Yes, death is round about us everywhere. Even the animals and plants die.

Why is it that one day, unless Jesus Christ returns first, my body will be placed in a casket and lowered into a hole in the earth? Why is it that the body in which I live, and which has served me well, will one day turn to dust?

We must go back to the book of Genesis, for there we have the story of creation and the sin of our ancestors, Adam and Eve.

Adam was placed in the Garden of Eden to rule God's creation where there was no death, because there was no sin. However, our ancestor Adam was not just our ancestor; he was our representative in that beautiful creation and the way that he reacted to God's law would have an effect upon every person who ever lived.

God told Adam, 'Of every tree of the garden you may freely eat; but of the tree of the knowledge of good and evil you shall not eat, for in the day that you eat of it you shall surely die' (Genesis 2:16-17).

The visible sign of Adam's sin was that his body began ageing. We see this effect of sin in our own bodies and those of others. The wrinkles appear, the hearing becomes more difficult, sight begins to fade, hair turns grey and sometimes falls out, leaving the person bald. We suffer aches and pains from a variety of sicknesses and eventually death claims us.

No longer was life wonderful in God's earthly paradise, as Adam and Eve were ordered out of the Garden of Eden on the day they sinned and from that day onwards they found work to be hard labour. God said to Adam:

In the sweat of your face you shall eat bread
Till you return to the ground,
For out of it you were taken;
For dust you are,
And to dust you shall return

(Genesis 3:19).

Adam died and so did Eve and, with the exception of Enoch and Elijah, so has every person born upon this earth. Even the Lord Jesus Christ died because he was the representative of his people and he endured the punish-

147

ment due to their sin. After being nailed to a cross he died. His body was then taken down from the cross and placed in a tomb. Yes, the Lord Jesus Christ really died!

Physical death is our enemy. In fact Paul wrote, 'For he [Christ] must reign till he has put all enemies under his feet. The last enemy that will be destroyed is death' (1 Corinthians 15:25-26).

While Christians may not fear dying, the process of dying can be very unpleasant in some situations. However, we can rest in the promise of God that he will never desert us, no matter what the circumstances might be. Like King David, we shall be able to say,

Yea, though I walk through the valley of the shadow of death,
I will fear no evil; for you are with me;
Your rod and your staff, they comfort me

(Psalm 23:4).

He will be there to smooth the pillow and his angels will be waiting at our bedside to escort our soul into the presence of the Lord Jesus Christ. In Psalm 116:15 we read, 'Precious in the sight of the LORD is the death of his saints.'

Death to the Christian means being with the Lord, so all Christians should be able to say, 'Amen' to Paul's words: 'For to me, to live is Christ, and to die is gain' (Philippians 1:21).

Death is not the end. The grave does not have the victory because one day the dead will rise again. We can be certain of this because that is exactly what Jesus Christ did. Paul argued that because Christ rose from the dead he is the first-fruits of all who have died in him.

And what wonderful bodies all of Christ's people will have on that day! The Scriptures declare: 'The body ... is sown in dishonour, it is raised in glory. It is sown in weakness, it is raised in power. It is sown a natural body, it is raised a spiritual body' (1 Corinthians 15:43-44). Our glorified bodies will be reunited with our souls, which will have been made perfectly holy and free at last from every taint of sin.

All who belong to Christ will only die once. Are you among that number? You can know that you are if you have come to Christ in faith, with genuine repentance for your sins, and if you are now seeking to show your love for him by living as one of his faithful followers.

To think about
•••

1. Only two people in the history of the world did not die. Who were they?

2. What happens to a person when he or she dies?

3. Think carefully about this question: Two people in the world's history did not die — will there ever be others who do not die? (Read 1 Corinthians 15:50-57 if you are not sure of the answer.)

The second death

Read
••••••••••••••••••••
Revelation 20:7-15

'Then Death and Hades were cast into the lake of fire. This is the second death. And anyone not found written in the Book of Life was cast into the lake of fire' (Revelation 20:14-15).

I have stood beside an open grave where I have heard someone say of a departed person who gave no evidence of being a Christian, 'Poor old ...! He's out of his pain and troubles now!'

If there was only one death I could agree with such a statement, but the Bible tells me that there is a second death. The Scriptures are full of warnings that there is a place called hell, a place of eternal punishment for all who live and die without Christ.

When God warned Adam that sin would bring death, two types of death were spoken of: the first was the death of the body which we thought about in the previous chapter; the second was spiritual death.

The moment Adam and Eve sinned the fellowship that existed between God and man in Eden came to an end. Man died spiritually. No longer was Adam inclined to do what was good in God's sight, but sin affected every part of his humanity. Man was now spiritually dead, unable and unwilling to reach out his hand towards God. No longer was God the centre of man's universe, but man became a god to himself.

Hanging over the head of every human being was the justice of God which had to be satisfied. Man was to be punished for sin and God's punishment for all who are not living by faith in Christ is the second death. The psalmist tells us very plainly that 'God is angry with the wicked every day' (Psalm 7:11).

The apostle John wrote about the second death in the book of Revelation. He described the scene where all humans were standing before the judgement throne: 'And they were judged, each one according to his works. Then Death and Hades were cast into the lake of fire. This is the second death. And anyone not found written in the Book of Life was cast into the lake of fire' (Revelation 20:13-15).

The second death is hell, the place of eternal punishment. Again John wrote of this terrible place of punishment, 'And the smoke of their torment ascends for ever and ever; and they have no rest day or night...' (Revelation 14:11).

The story Christ told of the rich man and Lazarus paints a picture of the terror of the second death. We read of the rich man being sent to a place of torment, from where there was no way of escape (Luke 16:23-26).

The second death is called the lake of fire in Revelation 20. Elsewhere it is described differently, but each time the picture is of a hopeless situation. Hell is the bottomless pit (Revelation 9:2) and outer darkness. Jesus warned the Jews that their rejection of him as their Messiah would mean that the Gentiles would flock to him and find salvation. Then he went on to say, 'But the sons of the kingdom will be cast out into outer darkness. There will be weeping and gnashing of teeth' (Matthew 8:12). This again paints a picture of terror because the Jews of Christ's time believed evil spirits lived in darkness.

In our previous chapter where we looked at the first death, mention was made of the resurrection. Not only Christians will rise from the grave, but all the dead will rise again. The resurrection of unbelievers we are told will be to 'shame and everlasting contempt' (Daniel 12:2).

We shall all stand before the judgement-seat where we shall be asked to give an account of all we have done on earth. Those who belong to Christ, who have experienced the second birth, will be welcomed into his presence to enjoy him for ever. Those who are strangers to Christ will face the wrath of God and experience the truth that an angry God is 'a consuming fire' (Hebrews 12:29). The psalmist wrote that 'A fire goes before [the LORD], and burns up his enemies round about' (Psalm 97:3).

The Lord Jesus Christ spoke more about the second death than he did about heaven. This fact surely is a warning that hell is real and that sinners should come to Christ the Saviour for forgiveness and shelter before it is too late.

Many of the parables give very explicit warnings about the fires of hell. The parable of the wheat and the tares is such a one. Christ declared that at the end of the age he would send forth his angels to gather the ungodly together and 'cast them into the furnace of fire. There will be wailing and gnashing of teeth' (Matthew 13:42).

Finally, all who profess faith in Christ need to examine their faith to ensure it is a living faith. Jesus said, 'Not everyone who says to me, "Lord, Lord," shall enter the kingdom of heaven, but he who does the will of my Father in heaven. Many will say to me in that day, "Lord, Lord, have we not prophesied in your name, cast out demons in your name, and done many wonders in your name?" And then I will declare to them, "I never knew you; depart from me, you who practise lawlessness!" ' (Matthew 7:21-23).

It is my hope and prayer that none of those who read these words will ever experience that second death.

To think about

1. What is the second death, and why is it to be feared?
2. Who will experience the second death?
3. How can the second death be avoided?
4. Look back to the words you read in Matthew 7:21-23. What do they teach you?

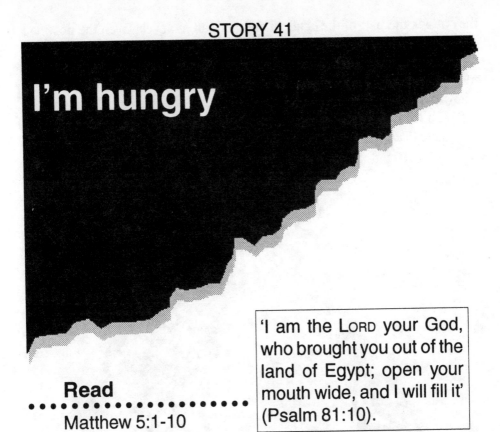

I'm hungry

Read

Matthew 5:1-10

'I am the LORD your God, who brought you out of the land of Egypt; open your mouth wide, and I will fill it' (Psalm 81:10).

Magpies are very common in Australia. Early in the morning we can hear them warbling high up in the trees. I think they sound beautiful. However, my brother John, who now lives in a large city, always complains about being woken up early in the morning when staying at our home, by the sounds of magpies warbling, cocks crowing and dogs barking. When I stay at his home in the city I would love to be awakened by such sounds. Instead I wake up to the sound of traffic roaring past, sirens screeching and the noise of trains. I would rather have the sound of the birds any day!

Magpies have some bad habits. During nesting-time they act like dive-bombers. They are very territorial and always want to keep people away from their nests, which means that if anyone walks too close to the tree where they are nesting they attack. They fly down like a dive-bomber and without warning peck the intruder on the head. They always attack from behind and usually the first thing the person hears is the flurry of wings as the birds grab at the hair on his head. Then away they fly while their victim runs for his life. When he is on the run they usually attack a second time. So during magpie nesting-time in Australia many children walk to school waving a stick in the air, just to keep the magpies away. Some people go to the trouble of wearing white ice-cream containers on their heads, with a pair of eyes painted on the back. They believe this will keep the magpies away as they attack the part of the head where there are no eyes. Even the postman delivering mail is watchful for the magpies.

When the eggs are hatched the babies demand food. They open their mouths and start squawking for their parents to bring them their dinner. They love worms and grubs and Mum and Dad Magpie must find it a full-time job finding enough food to satisfy all the hungry babies. Even when they have been fed the squawking only stops for a short time.

I guess all babies are the same. I can remember our children crying for milk when they were young. Even Wags barks at us when his food tray is empty. If he wants something to eat and his dish is empty he sits beside it and barks till we come. Sometimes, when he tires of waiting for us to come, he brings his dish to us, drops it at our feet and then barks.

In today's text God speaks in a wonderful way to his people Israel who had been rescued from the land of Egypt. God called upon his people to be faithful to him. They were warned not to follow the gods of the nations around them. In fact God invited the people to open their mouths like the hungry animals and he would fill them. They were promised ideal growing conditions which would produce the best crops imaginable. In this psalm Asaph said, speaking of God, 'He would have fed them also with the finest of wheat; and with honey from the rock I would have satisfied you' (Psalm 81:16). God would have kept the nation safe from their enemies and the people would have lived in peace. How sad it is to read, 'But my people would not heed my voice, and Israel would have none of me'! (Psalm 81:11).

God invited the people to open their spiritual mouths and had they responded he would have blessed them with a greater love for himself, but they wanted to worship and serve foreign gods. Israel cast off God and he in turn cast them off. When the Jews crucified Christ, the gospel was taken to the Gentiles — to you and me. We must all thank God for his goodness to each one of us if we are saved by the precious shed blood of our Saviour Jesus Christ.

In the passage set for today's reading we learn about the character of a Christian. And in that passage from the Sermon on the Mount we find some words similar in meaning to today's text: 'Blessed are those who hunger and thirst for righteousness, for they shall be filled' (Matthew 5:6). All who love God and serve the Lord Jesus Christ should be like those hungry baby magpies that opened their mouths and squawked for food from their mother and father. Just as their parents feed them with delicious worms until they can eat no more, so it is with Christ's people. We cry out for spiritual food that we might serve the Lord Jesus better, and when we pray to God in this way, he hears us and fills us with his righteousness.

We are fed when we read the Bible, or hear the pastor preach from the Scriptures. You are even fed by reading these stories. But the Holy Spirit must take the spiritual food and apply it to our souls. Then we shall be satisfied. We shall then be able to serve Christ as we should. If you do not seek to be fed by God you will end up suffering from spiritual malnutrition and become stunted in your spiritual growth. Don't allow this to happen to you!

Let us cry out to God for righteousness and God will honour his promise — our (spiritual) mouths will be filled.

To think about

1. We need food to keep our bodies functioning. What are the good foods you should be eating?
2. What spiritual food do you need to keep your spiritual life going? How do you get that spiritual food?
3. Read Matthew 5:6 and discuss what it is teaching.
4. How best can Mum and Dad spiritually feed their children?

The dog sat on the tucker-box

Read
••••••••••••••••••••
Revelation 2:8-11

> 'Therefore know that the LORD your God, he is God, the faithful God who keeps covenant and mercy for a thousand generations with those who love him and keep his commandments...' (Deuteronomy 7:9).

We all admire dependable people. People who let us down do not usually become our good friends. If you play a sport, you know you depend upon the other members of the team, just as they depend upon you. Your parents expect to be able to rely on you and I'm sure you rely on them. Faithfulness is an important ingredient of life.

Each nation of the world has stories about faithful animals and I know that dogs feature in many of those stories. I would like to tell you a story about a special dog.

On the highway between Melbourne and Sydney you will find a statue of a dog sitting on a food-box, which Australians call a tucker-box. If any of my overseas readers ever visit Australia and travel the Hume Highway, keep an eye out for Gundagai. The new highway bypasses this country town, but the statue for which the town is well known has been moved to a spot beside the bypass where travellers can stop and have a look at it. So popular is the story about the dog sitting on the tucker-box that we have a song which includes the line: 'The dog sits on the tucker-box, nine miles from Gundagai.'

In the early days following white settlement in Australia great flocks of sheep were cared for by drovers. The life of the drover was hard, but they always had their own cook who travelled with them and the flock of sheep. All the men had their own dogs who worked hard to keep the sheep under control. Even the cook had his dog. The famous Gundagai dog belonged to the cook. He had trained his dog to keep watch over the drovers' food which he kept in a large tucker-box. I imagine there was always the problem of a drover sneaking up and stealing some of the food. But the cook's dog made sure no one touched the food in the box. When the cook was absent the dog would sit on the lid of the box and keep the food safe.

Tuckerbox

One day the cook left his dog on guard, walked away into the bush and died there. The faithful dog just sat on the tucker-box and waited for his master to return. I imagine that that evening, when the cook had not come back, the drovers went looking for him while some tried to prepare the evening meal. However, the dog refused to move. He knew what his job was and he was staying at his post till his master returned! And it was there beside that tucker-box that the faithful dog finally died, waiting for the return of his human friend who never came back.

Our text tells us a wonderful truth — our God is a faithful God, who always keeps his promises. He will never let his people down! As you read the Scriptures you discover that they are filled with evidences of God's faithfulness. God promised to send a Saviour, and he did. God promises to save all who trust themselves to his Son, the Lord Jesus Christ, and he does. Jesus has promised that if we confess our sins he will forgive us and totally cleanse us (1 John 1:9), and he does! God has also given his word that all who refuse to repent of their sins will be sent to hell, and that too will happen. God's faithfulness cannot be questioned because he is always true to his word.

Our God demands that we in turn remain faithful to him. When we are born again God takes hold of us and promises that he will never let us go.

This means he gives us the grace to remain faithful to him. We may fall into sin, but he makes repentance possible.

In our reading we are told that the Christians in the church at Smyrna were about to be persecuted by the unbelieving Jews, who had put Christ to death and hated all his disciples. However, Jesus told his people not to fear when they were persecuted. He told them that some would be thrown into prison, while others would be put to death. Then he gave a wonderful promise: 'Be faithful unto death, and I will give you the crown of life' (Revelation 2:10). There was no hell waiting for those devoted saints. When the persecution commenced these loyal Christians would have remembered Christ's promises and have drawn from them courage to remain faithful to their Saviour.

Now, how about you? Are you a Christian? If so, do you show your faith by being obedient to God, no matter what others say or do to you? May you all be loyal servants of Christ and then God will give you the crown of life.

To think about
• •

1. Our text speaks of God as one who 'keeps covenant'. What does this mean?

2. List some of God's covenants made with humans.

3. What is the 'new covenant' spoken about in the New Testament?

4. Christians are called upon to be faithful to Christ. What does this mean? And what is the 'crown of life' that God has promised to his people?

Chasing your tail is a waste of time

Read
• • • • • • • • • • • • • • • • • • •
Ecclesiastes 12:6-14

' "Vanity of vanities," says the Preacher, "All is vanity" ' (Ecclesiastes 12:8).

If we all kept a record of how we spent our time during one week we would be surprised at the amount of time we wasted. Much of our time is spent sleeping, of course, but when we are up and about are we spending our time in a sensible way? Whatever we do, we must do it as we would if we were working for the Lord Jesus (see Colossians 3:23-24). This means we must always do our best and only do those things that are pleasing to our Saviour. Time is a gift of God to us and should never be wasted, but we do all waste so much of our time.

My dog is a great time-waster. He spends a lot of time lying on his bed in the sun. But I think his greatest time-wasting activity is chasing his tail. When Wags catches a glimpse of his tail, which is usually curled up over his back and covered with long hair, his eyes open wide and around he goes spinning about in a circle, teeth snapping at the hair which most of the time is a couple of centimetres out of reach. He keeps up the chase for minutes and sometimes collapses in a heap on the ground. On other occasions he trips over his feet or bumps into something and again ends up in a heap. Then he starts the chase all over again. Val and I just watch him and laugh. I know Wags thinks it is great fun chasing his tail, but it is all a waste of time. If he ever manages to catch his tail he never seems to know what to do with it. He hangs on tightly, comes to a standstill and there he stands or sits, with

159

his mouth around the end of his tail. His eyes look to us as if to say, 'I've caught it, but what do I do now?'

Many people spend a lifetime doing things that are a waste of time. They chase money, or power, or possessions, or just the good life. Maybe they achieve their goals, but at the end of life, if Christ is not their Lord and Saviour, everything they have done will prove to have been a waste of time.

Every person who loves Christ has one great aim in life: to live in a way that is pleasing to him. We must work in order to provide for our own needs and those of our family. The apostle Paul wrote, 'If anyone does not provide for his own, and especially for those of his household, he has denied the faith and is worse than an unbeliever' (1 Timothy 5:8). We are never to deliberately allow ourselves to become financial burdens to other people, or the government. Paul said, 'If anyone will not work, neither shall he eat' (2 Thessalonians 3:10).

We must also support the work of ministry. The fact is that our hard-earned money is not just ours to do with as we please. We must never allow money to be our goal in life.

Paul writes that we must use our opportunities to serve one another (Galatians 5:13). This we must do willingly and cheerfully remembering that in all we do, we are serving the Lord (Colossians 3:23-24) out of love for him.

Of course we all need to relax at times. Jesus called his disciples to come away with him for a time and rest (Mark 6:31). They had been working very hard and they needed rest to refresh themselves for further service. There is no sin in having a rest or a well-earned holiday.

But someone might ask, 'And what about the sport I play? Is that pleasing to God?' The answer is, 'Yes, if you play the game according to the rules.' Again it is Paul who tells us that 'Bodily exercise profits a little' (1 Timothy 4:8). Exercise keeps our bodies healthy so we can be of greater use in the Lord's service. We can enjoy the good things that God has given us, but let us never be silly enough to act like a dog chasing its own tail — to do those things that have no value whatever.

The most important matter of all is found in our reading: 'Remember ... your Creator', and the time to start is while you are young (Ecclesiastes 12:1). It is sad but true that the older people become, the less likely they are to turn to God and seek forgiveness. Our reading warns us that the day is coming when everything will be revealed, both the good and evil things we have done.

Let us not be like Wags who wastes so much time chasing his tail. The Lord spoke of people who set and achieved their godless goals: 'For what shall it profit a man if he gains the whole world, and loses his own soul?' (Mark 8:36).

Serve the Lord in all you do. Enjoy God's wonderful creation and look forward to the day when you will see Christ face to face. On Judgement Day all that will matter is our relationship to Christ. Make sure that you have made that your greatest priority during your life on earth and that you really are trusting him for your salvation. Seek to serve him out of love and gratitude to him for all he has done for you.

To think about
● ●

1. How much time do you waste each day?
2. Make a list of reasons why people work day after day. Are some of these reasons not really sensible?
3. Ecclesiastes 12:1 says, 'Remember your Creator...' What does this mean?

He had one good friend

Read
• •
John 15:9-17

'A man who has friends must himself be friendly, but there is a friend who sticks closer than a brother' (Proverbs 18:24).

It is good to have friends. Some people complain that they have no friends but they have only themselves to blame as they do not show friendliness to others. How can they expect others to be friends with them? We win friends by being friendly to others.

Many years ago a nice young man called at our home. His name was David and he had met our daughter Heather at secondary school. I guess they had felt some attraction for one another, because David kept coming

back to see her and eventually they decided to get married. David also made friends with the rest of the family. He went out of his way to win Val's friendship by giving her chocolates and flowers. Sometimes he used to come fishing with me. Even Sox the cat became David's friend. Often when David visited us, Heather would try to sit beside him, but the cat would come and snuggle down between the two of them. Yes, Sox and David were good friends.

162

Eventually the day arrived when David and Heather were to be married. All the plans were made, everything was ready, everyone was excited and we all had our best clothes waiting to be put on for the big day.

Some of David's Christian friends decided to take him out for a meal on the night before the wedding. They were a friendly group of young men and I know they enjoyed their evening together. After David and Heather returned from their honeymoon, he asked if he had kept us awake on the night before the wedding. He hadn't, but I wanted to know the reason for the question.

He then told us what had happened. After the Chinese meal, David's brother produced a chain and a padlock and the group of young men then drove David to our home where they chained him to the tow-bar of our car. Then they drove away, leaving David to sort out his problem.

I asked, 'Why didn't you call out and let us help you?'

But David hadn't wanted to wake everyone up so he stood there, with the mosquitoes biting him, wondering what he should do. Then there ap-

peared a good friend. Sox had heard the noise and came to investigate. David said the cat rubbed himself against his legs and meowed, indicating that he wanted to be picked up and cuddled. David was left for a couple of hours with his good friend Sox, who refused to leave him. Some time later, David's brother returned and released him so he could get a few hours' sleep.

It is good to have friends. Friends are spoken about many times in the Bible.

I think one of the most wonderful uses of the word 'friend' is where the Bible speaks of a person being a friend of God. In the book of James we read of Abraham, who truly trusted God and was called 'the friend of God' (James 2:23). In Isaiah 41:8 we read that God described him as 'Abraham my friend'. Abraham was a friend of the living God and he showed this by loving God day after day and obeying his commandments. God blessed Abraham in many wonderful ways.

Now comes the important question: 'Are you a friend of God?' Your friendship with God depends upon your friendship with the Lord Jesus Christ. If you are trusting in Christ alone for your salvation you are indeed his friend. If you have a saving faith in Christ you will show it by keeping his commandments and doing those things which please him.

Jesus declared in John 15:13 that he had laid down his life for his friends, which is the greatest sign of love possible. But then he went on to say: 'You are my friends if you do whatever I command you' (v. 14). Obedience to Christ is the great sign that we are his friends. What a wonderful thing it is to be called a friend of Jesus Christ, who is God! He is our Elder Brother and Friend who stands beside us throughout life and all eternity. He will never let us down.

During his life on earth Jesus showed great friendship to sinners. He ate and drank with them and the scribes and Pharisees mocked him for doing so. Many of those people became followers of Christ. We too must show friendship to those who do not yet know the Lord, and that friendship might well be used by the Holy Spirit to bring them to a saving faith in Jesus Christ, the Friend of sinners. However, we must be careful not to let ourselves be led by our non-Christian friends into doing or saying anything which is not pleasing to our heavenly Friend, the Lord Jesus Christ.

To think about

1. Name a couple of your close friends and talk about what makes a person a good friend.
2. It is God who chooses his friends and makes it possible for us to have him as our heavenly Father. How do we show Christ that we are his friends?
3. How did Christ show sinners that he could be their Friend?

Who is the head of the church?

Read
• • • • • • • • • • • • • • • • •
Colossians 1:13-18

'And he put all things under his feet, and gave him to be head over all things to the church, which is his body...' (Ephesians 1:22-23).

The Scriptures are very clear that there is only one head of the church and that is our Saviour, the Lord Jesus Christ. Many Christians have laid down their lives rather than acknowledge any other head for the church. In the United Kingdom many years ago, in the reigns of King Charles II and his brother James II (James VII of Scotland), a large number of Scots laid down their lives when the king demanded that everyone acknowledge him as the head of the church. I would like to tell you in more detail the story of the two women whom I mentioned in story 33 who were put to death by the English soldiers because they would not bow to the demands of the king.

These two women, Margaret Wilson, who was only eighteen, and Margaret M'Lauchlan, a woman of about seventy years of age,[1] were told that if they refused to acknowledge the king as head of the church they would be put to death. Both ladies were willing to die rather than to deny their Saviour. The method of execution was very cruel — both women were to be tied to stakes well out on the shores of Wigtown Bay in the Solway Firth (a river estuary which forms the boundary between south-west Scotland and the north-west of England). They were to be left there until the incoming tide drowned them.

On 11 May 1685, a day in late spring, a crowd gathered on the shore to witness the execution. The two women stood bravely together while the

165

stakes were put in place. Then the older woman, Margaret M'Lauchlan, was tied to her stake and everyone watched as the waters crept up around her body. The cruel soldiers thought that Margaret Wilson would change her mind and say she acknowledged that the king was head of the church when she saw the suffering of her friend. However, Margaret Wilson loved her Lord and, like many others, decided that death was to be preferred to turning her back upon Christ.

Soon young Margaret too was bound to the stake and the cold waters began to creep up around her body. In the short time left before her death she read the wonderful words of Romans 8. I feel sure that the Holy Spirit gave her great comfort and courage as she read, 'Who shall separate us from the love of Christ? Shall tribulation, or distress, or persecution, or famine, or nakedness, or peril, or sword? As it is written: "For your sake we are killed all day long; we are accounted as sheep for the slaughter." Yet in all these things we are more than conquerors through him who loved us...' (Romans 8:35-36).

She went on to sing the metrical version of Psalm 25, beginning at verse 7:

My sins and faults of youth,
Do thou, O Lord, forget;
After thy mercy think on me,
And for thy goodness great...

Then Margaret bowed her head in prayer as the waters swirled around her, almost covering her head. However, the soldiers suddenly grabbed hold

of her in those last minutes and lifted her head clear of the water. They asked her once more to renounce Christ as head of the church and said that if she did she could go free. Margaret's reply before they cruelly pushed her back under the water to drown was: 'I will not! I am one of Christ's children; let me go!'

And so died two faithful servants of the Lord Jesus Christ. There is one Head of the church, the Lord Jesus Christ. In some churches today we find a man or woman who claims to be the head of the church. The pope of Rome is the best-known example. He claims to be supreme ruler of the church but this cannot be, for the Scriptures speak of Christ and the church in these words: 'And he [Christ] is the head of the body, the church, who is the beginning, the firstborn from the dead, that in all things he may have the pre-eminence' (Colossians 1:18).

When we go to church we need to remember that we worship the God and Father of the one who is the Head of the church, the Lord Jesus Christ — King Jesus!

I pray that none of us will ever be called upon to face death because of our faithfulness to Christ, but remember that if this should happen to any of us our Lord will give us the courage and strength we need to face all that the enemy might do to us. Just as the two Margarets bravely died for their Lord, so Christ will enable all of his people who are called to be martyrs to face death with courage and trust in him.

May God make us strong, faithful members of the kingdom of King Jesus.

1. Her gravestone gives her age as sixty-three, but a petition which she herself addressed to the Privy Council shortly before her death gave it as about seventy.

To think about
●●

1. There is only one 'head' of the church. Who is that head?
2. There have been and still are people who claim to be the 'head' of the church. Who are they and how do they show themselves to be that 'head'?
3. If Christ is the 'head' of the church, what are the people who believe in him?
4. Always remember that Jesus Christ is the King of the church; he has given us his laws and we must obey. Read your Bible each day so you will understand more about his kingdom and the laws you must obey.

Treasure in pieces of clay

> 'But we have this treasure in earthen vessels, that the excellence of the power may be of God and not of us' (2 Corinthians 4:7).

Read
• • • • • • • • • • • • • • • • • •
2 Corinthians 4:1-15

My brother John rang me one day to tell me of a wedding he conducted some time ago. He was laughing and said that at the wedding breakfast the bridegroom messed up his speech. The poor man stood up beside his new wife and began to speak. He thanked everyone for coming along and for their gifts and then began to speak about the beautiful girl sitting beside him. However, instead of saying nice things about his new wife, he spent most of the time talking about her lovely wedding clothes. He pointed to her jewellery that sparkled in the light

and said it looked beautiful. Then he spoke about her stunning gown and veil. John said he even mentioned the satin shoes she wore.

Then the bride stood up and said, 'Yes, the clothes are great, but he didn't say anything about me!' She then spoke glowingly about the kind man she had married. She didn't even mention his well-cut, new suit. Clothes are important, but what really matters is what the person inside the clothes is like.

When John found his first nugget of gold it was in the middle of a lump of clay. When he eventually held the gold in his hand he thought of our text for today. However, he made a mistake with his magnificent golden nugget. He bought a very smart container to hold his precious piece of gold. When he showed it to his friends everyone commented about the lovely case as it looked more precious than the gold. For a short time afterwards John carried his nugget around in an old leather bag hanging from his neck. Most people have never seen a lump of gold and say how great it looks when John holds it in his hand. When people pick it up for a closer look John keeps a close watch on where it goes.

Our text and reading speak of a great treasure that is found in vessels of clay. That treasure is Christ and the glorious gospel of salvation which is to be found in him. The gospel is carried about in vessels of clay — that is, by human beings. We are made of the dust of the earth and have the glorious truths of Christ in our hearts. It is men and women who speak to others of Christ and glorify the Redeemer. Elsewhere Paul said that he preached the gospel in plain language and often was filled with godly fear as he did so. Writing to the Corinthians he said, 'I was with you in weakness, in fear, and in much trembling. And my speech and my preaching were not with persuasive words of human wisdom, but in demonstration of the Spirit and of power' (1 Corinthians 2:3-4).

In our reading Paul tells us that the gospel is contained in bodies that are dying. He had suffered greatly as he went from city to city preaching Christ crucified. Paul knew that one day his body would die, but it would be raised anew — just like the glorious, resurrected body of his Saviour.

It is the gospel that brings spiritual life to sinners. Pastors and others who preach the gospel are rarely the most glamorous of men, nor do they dress up in the smartest or most expensive clothing. They do not have to use fancy words. But what a great privilege it is for human beings to be those who carry the gospel of salvation in Christ to others! When vessels of clay preach Christ all the glory goes to the Lord.

Of course, pastors and preachers have special responsibilities for bringing the gospel to others, but all of us who are Christians have the privilege of telling others the precious truths about what the Lord Jesus has done for us, and so of bringing glory to his name.

If any of my readers are not Christians, may the Lord be pleased to use the witness of Christians whom you know, and even of books like this one, to bring you to repentance from your sins and faith in Christ as your Lord and Saviour.

To think about ....

1. It is usually just ordinary people who witness to the saving work of the Lord Jesus Christ. Why is this so?
2. Paul speaks about the 'treasure in earthen vessels'. What is the 'treasure' and what is the 'earthen vessel' he speaks about?
3. Why can we say that we are 'earthen vessels'?

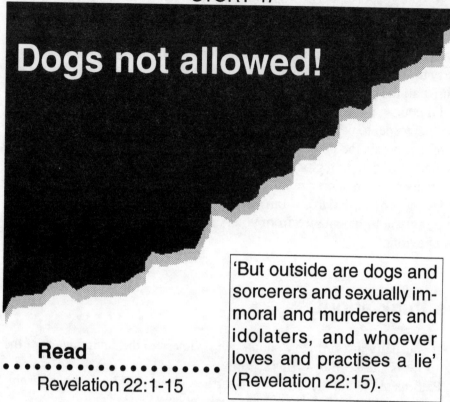

Dogs not allowed!

Read

•••••••••••••••••••

Revelation 22:1-15

'But outside are dogs and sorcerers and sexually immoral and murderers and idolaters, and whoever loves and practises a lie' (Revelation 22:15).

Recently Val and I went away for a short holiday and Wags came along too. He doesn't like being left behind when we go outside our front door because he knows that he is part of our family and should always be with us, wherever we go. When he sees us dressing for town he follows us everywhere. He doesn't want to miss out on anything. If he is outside and hears the windows being locked he runs inside and looks up at us as if to say, 'I know you're going away. Please take me with you.' When we come home after leaving him locked inside the house, many times he sulks and refuses to have anything to do with us for hours.

As we were going away for two weeks we thought it unfair to expect our children and grandchildren to look after Wags, even though they would have loved it. So Wags came too. In another story I told you about his behaviour when we were stopped by a policeman.

Eventually we arrived at the holiday cottage and settled in. That night we slept to the sound of the waves breaking on the shore. After our long drive we needed a good night's sleep. Early in the morning Wags was ready for a day's activities, so down to the beach we walked. Val and I enjoyed quietly paddling in the water and getting the sand between our toes but Wags went berserk. This was his first visit to the seaside so he ran down to the water's edge, where he spent some time running about as the waves crashed on the sand. Eventually he was in the water and proved to be a great dog-paddler!

As we were returning to our holiday cottage we saw the sign at the entrance to the beach: 'No dogs allowed.' Beside the words was a drawing of a black dog with a line through him. I said, 'Wags is white, so he'll be all right!' However, we knew the sign really applied to all dogs, so we had to find another beach where Wags could have a run on the sand and a swim in the sea.

'No dogs allowed!' That sign is the same as we find attached to the gates into heaven. No dogs may enter there! Read today's text.

Not every person will enter heaven, but only those who belong to Christ and demonstrate this by a life of obedience to him. When God's people enter heaven they will be completed clothed in the holiness of the Lord Jesus Christ, their representative and substitute. Those who have have never trusted in Christ as their Saviour are not permitted to enter. 'No dogs enter heaven.' Of course we need to ask what is meant by the word 'dogs'.

The dogs spoken of here are not pet dogs like my dear little Wags. When Christ lived on the earth wild dogs roamed the streets eating whatever they could. Many people threw their rubbish and food scraps out onto the roadside and the wild dogs, who roamed about in packs, scavenged through the rubbish finding food to eat. No one loved dogs like that, and they were friends with nobody. They were not invited into people's homes. In Christ's days, people might well have had a sign on the front gate which read: 'No dogs allowed!'

The dogs spoken of in Revelation 22:15 are all those people who are unclean, who do not live according to God's law. They are the people who lead others astray by teaching falsehood; they are the immoral people of the world who have never repented of their sins.

In the previous verse we read, 'Blessed are those who do his commandments, that they may have the right to the tree of life, and may enter through the gates into the city.' The people who obey the commandments of Christ and do so because they love him will find the doorway to heaven opened. They will be allowed to enter into Christ's presence. Outside are the 'dogs' — the unrepentant, sinful people.

I hope that all of my readers are among those who love God and are faithful servants of the Lord Jesus. If so, one day we shall see the face of Christ, and the name of our Saviour will be ours for ever — we shall belong to Christ. What a wonderful future lies before each one of Christ's people!

But how dreadful it will be for those who are shut out of God's presence for ever! If you have never repented of your sins and called on Christ to save you, I urge you to do so before it is too late!

To think about
••

1. Who will be allowed to enter heaven?
2. When we read the sign in the Bible telling us, 'Dogs not allowed', what are we being taught concerning those not permitted to enter heaven?
3. Where and what is heaven?
4. What do you think will be the most wonderful thing about heaven?

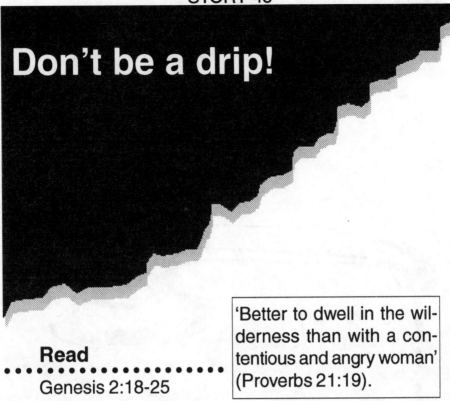

Don't be a drip!

Read

Genesis 2:18-25

'Better to dwell in the wilderness than with a contentious and angry woman' (Proverbs 21:19).

There are many different family groups in our world. In Western society we usually think of a family as made up of a mum, a dad and children. However, in our family there are just two of us, Val and me (and Wags!). Our reading tells us that as Adam could find no one in creation to be a wife and companion to him, God made a woman to be his wife. He made Eve from Adam's rib and together they lived in a perfect world. At first there was no sin or death and Adam and Eve were perfectly happy together. It was only when sin entered the world that trouble between husbands and wives started.

To be part of a happy family is a great privilege and if you are in such a family, thank God for what he has done for you.

When we built our house we could not agree for some time about the roof that we wanted. I thought an iron roof would be great as I have always loved the sound of rain falling on the roof, but Val wisely said, 'No, we should have tiles, as they last a lifetime.' I finally agreed and we have a tiled roof, but I miss the sound of rain falling on the roof.

A couple of nights ago I woke up to the sound of a dripping tap. Now isn't it strange? I like the sound of rain falling on the roof, but I can't stand the sound of a dripping tap. For a time I lay in bed waiting for the next drip to fall. Then I started counting the number of seconds between the drips. Finally I crawled out of bed — but not before first waking Val and asking

her if she could hear the dripping noise. When she was fully awake she said, 'Yes, I can hear it. But why did you wake me up?'

So I put a piece of rag under the spot where the drips were falling and went back to bed where I finally fell asleep. The next day, the first thing I did was replace the tap washer. Now I can sleep soundly.

The Bible has something to say about wives who are always angry and complaining. We read, 'A continual dripping on a very rainy day and a contentious woman are alike' (Proverbs 27:15). Solomon, who wrote most of the book of Proverbs, should have known about this as we are told he had 700 wives as well as other women in his harem!

I have my own special room, my study. In this room I have all my books, my computer, files, Asian masks and paintings I like hanging on the wall, a bed and all the bits and pieces I need for my writing.

Solomon gave husbands some good advice when he wrote, '[It is] better to dwell in a corner of a housetop, than in a house shared with a contentious woman' (Proverbs 21:9). If Val was an angry and nagging wife I would live in the study.

Solomon did not only complain about nagging wives but irritable husbands, for he also said, 'As charcoal is to burning coals, and wood to fire, so is a contentious man to kindle strife' (Proverbs 26:21). And I'm sure that if Val found me to be an irritable husband she would keep out of my way.

When we went on holiday, Val commented that Wags was a good traveller and never once did he complain and say, 'I'm tired. How far have we to go?' He slept most of the time. Children can spoil the peace of the family by complaining and being a continual nuisance. In fact every family member must play his or her part to make the home a place of peace and contentment. It is so easy for family members to shatter the peace of the home. Children are to obey their parents, and parents are not to do things to deliberately upset their children.

We all have the responsibility to be good family members, which requires effort. I hope your family gathers each day for family worship. There is a saying that 'The family that prays together, stays together.' This is not always the case, but husbands and wives need to remember that if they are both Christians they do not just live together, but that they are 'heirs together of the grace of life' (1 Peter 3:7).

Married couples are to help one another grow spiritually. Husbands are to love their wives, 'just as Christ also loved the church and gave himself for her'. And wives are told to be 'submit', or ' be subject' to their husbands

(Ephesians 5:22-25). This does not mean that the wife must be the husband's slave. However, it does mean that there are times when the wife must accept the husband's decision, even though she doesn't agree. In homes where the teaching of God's Word on marriage is put into practice, husbands and wives talk through the decisions that must be made and usually this means a decision is made with which both can live and which is agreeable to both.

I think the great Bible commentator Matthew Henry said something that makes good sense: 'That the woman was made of a rib out of the side of Adam; not made out of his head to rule over him, nor out of his feet to be trampled upon by him, but out of his side to be equal with him, under his arm to be protected, and near his heart to be loved.' This sums up the type of relationship that should be found between husband and wife.

May we all play our part in making our family a happy place of peace and protection for all its members. Parents must set their children an example of a godly family life and children must be taught to respect each other.

In our world there is so much unhappiness in families, but let us remember that God's plan for humans was companionship and the ideal companionship is to be found in marriage. Marriages can work and homes can be made a place of happiness and contentment. I wouldn't swap Val for anything the world could offer. She is my friend and support and when she is absent I feel that part of me is missing. This is how it should be in all families, especially Christian families.

To think about
● ●

1. Make a list of the things that make you angry at home. Now compare lists and talk about the ways you can make living together a much more enjoyable experience.
2. Today, about half of all marriages end in divorce. What does this teach us about choosing a husband or a wife?
3. What can you do to make your community a better place for everyone?
4. How did Christ show his love for the church? What does this teach us all?

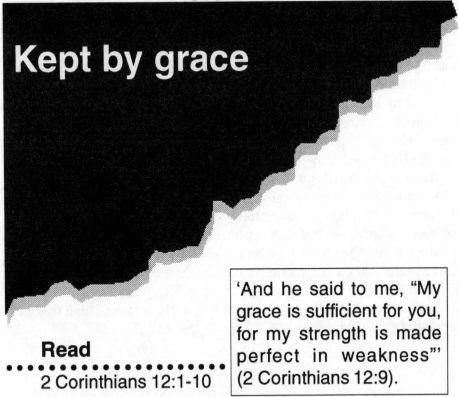

Kept by grace

Read

•••••••••••••••••••••
2 Corinthians 12:1-10

'And he said to me, "My grace is sufficient for you, for my strength is made perfect in weakness"' (2 Corinthians 12:9).

The apostle Paul had a problem which he called 'a thorn in the flesh' (2 Corinthians 12:7). I'm not sure what the problem was, but somehow I think it had something to do with his eyes. He wrote to the Galatians, 'For I bear you witness that, if possible, you would have plucked out your own eyes and given them to me' (Galatians 4:15). It may have been that Paul had an eye disease which spoilt his looks. No doubt this made his work of gospel preaching more difficult, as well as reading and writing his many letters. Whatever it was, Paul had a real problem which was of great concern to him.

So disturbed was he that he took his concern to the Lord in prayer. In fact we read that three times he pleaded with the Lord to have it removed. And what was the answer? Christ simply said, 'My grace is sufficient for you' (2 Corinthians 12:9). The Lord was saying that Paul would carry out all the work given to him and he would do it in the strength of his Saviour. So Paul continued to do the Lord's work, knowing that God was with him. And when he saw the great success which followed his preaching of the Word, he gave all the glory to God, who had worked through him.

All Christians depend daily upon the grace of God to carry out their duties and we should give all the glory to Christ for what we do. However, there are times when we think about events that are likely to take place in

179

our lives and wonder how we shall cope. Again the answer given to Paul in his difficulty is the one given to us: 'My grace is sufficient for you.'

Have you ever wondered how you will face death? Imagine what it will be like if one day a doctor says to you, 'There is nothing more I can do for you. You are going to die.' How will you feel and what will you do on that day? All I can say is that when that day arrives God will give you the grace you need to die. The God of peace will give you his peace, which is why Paul wrote, 'Be anxious for nothing, but in everything by prayer and supplication, with thanksgiving, let your requests be made known to God; and the peace of God, which surpasses all understanding, will guard your hearts and minds through Christ Jesus' (Philippians 4:6-7).

A young Scotsman by the name of Patrick Hamilton travelled to Wittenberg where he was taught the Reformed faith by Martin Luther and his friend Philip Melanchthon. When he returned to Scotland he began preaching the gospel. Soon he was taken prisoner, tried by the Roman Catholic Church authorities and sentenced to death. On the same day (28 February 1527) that young man, who was just twenty-four years old, was tied to a stake and burnt. He went to his death very bravely because Christ was with him and strengthened him.

Before he was tied to the stake he gave his outer clothing to a friend, telling him that he would have no need of it where he was going. When the fire was lit the bag of gunpowder tied to his body exploded, burning Patrick horribly. Then the flames began to die and go out. All the time Patrick stood firmly, suffering from severe burns and no doubt in great pain from his injuries, while the cruel men brought more gunpowder which made the flames once more flare up around his body. Then with the words, 'Lord Jesus receive my spirit', he passed away into the presence of Christ.

He did not shed tears, complain, or cry out for help. Why? Because the grace of God was sufficient to help him in that awful situation. Paul put it like this: 'For when I am weak, then I am strong' (2 Corinthians 12:10).

God's grace will be sufficient for each one of his people in every situation of their lives. Let us all seek to live for Christ and give him the glory for all he does for us.

But we must never forget that these promises are only for those who have been brought to see their need of a Saviour and are trusting in Christ, and Christ alone, for the forgiveness of their sins and their hope of heaven. Are you?

To think about
●●

1. We cannot be sure what Paul's 'thorn in the flesh' was, but we know that it caused him problems. Do you have any 'thorns in the flesh'?
2. The apostle Paul was at his very best when he faced difficulties. What did he mean when he said, 'For when I am weak, then I am strong'? (2 Corinthians 12:10).
3. Read today's text and explain what it teaches.
4. How can we cope when life becomes difficult?

Beware of the horse!

Read

. . . .

Deuteronomy 6:1-9

'Children, obey your parents in the Lord, for this is right' (Ephesians 6:1)

I have written several stories in my other books about John and me when we were young. Sometimes when we get together we talk about our 'growing-up days on the farm' and have a lot of laughs. Sometimes I am amazed that we both lived to tell those stories. There were some occasions when we disobeyed our parents and we look back to those times with shame.

God has commanded children to obey their parents. Usually Mum and Dad know a lot better than their children do, and the advice they give is for the children's good and safety. But if Mum or Dad ever asked you to do something that broke God's law (for example, to steal, or to tell a lie) you would have to politely say, 'No'.

The time had come for John to start school. I had been attending school for three years and to get to our school we had to ride bicycles. Now learning to ride a bike is sometimes a risky business. I'm sure, if you're a bike rider, you will remember the falls you had before you mastered your bicycle.

Well, the time came for John to learn to ride his new school bicycle. He had ridden mine many times, but now Mum and Dad had bought him his own new machine. It had a bell and back-pedal brake and looked shiny and sparkling in the sun. Dad put the bicycle beside mine in the hay-shed and said, 'Now, don't get on that bike till I come back.'

So there we stood beside a new bicycle. The temptation proved too great. 'Hop on, brother,' I suggested, 'and I'll give you a push. You can ride it before Dad gets back.' So John grabbed hold of his new bicycle and swung himself into the seat while I held on firmly.

Now our hay-shed was built above ground level and the track sloped downward towards the stables. It was a great place to ride bikes. We had a horse called Dick (Richard on Sunday!) who was usually very bad-tempered. When we went to put a bridle and saddle on him, often he would chase us around the paddock. He never chased Dad, but he knew he frightened both of us boys. Sometimes we ended up diving through the wires of the fence to escape being trampled by him. When he was tied up, often he would lash out with his foot when we came too close to him. We had to be very careful when we went riding on Dick because you never knew what he might do.

Well, John hopped on his bike. I held him firmly, and before I gave him a push we both checked to make sure Dad was not in sight. Dad didn't like to be disobeyed! I gave the bike a gentle push and off John went, wobbling

down the slope. Then I saw that Dick was tied up in the stable and there was my young brother wobbling his way straight towards the bad-tempered horse.

Now Dick had his back to us and we both expected him to lash out and knock John off his bike and maybe injure him. The horse looked around just as John rode between his two back legs. I know John was terrified because he gave a hideous whimper as he disappeared between the horse's legs.

At that very moment, Dad appeared on the scene and rushed towards John. Dick received the greatest fright of all. As the bike passed between his legs, he just hunched up his back and lowered his rear end. John fell off under Dick's belly!

So there stood Dick with a bike caught between his legs, tail down, legs bent, not knowing what was happening, with little John lying on the ground under him. John was up on his feet and out of there like a rocket just in time before Dick started kicking. He kicked so well that John's new bike had to be taken for repairs. New spokes had to be put in the front wheel and the paintwork had to be touched up.

184

Dad certainly wasn't smiling! We had disobeyed him and our disobedience had very nearly resulted in John's being badly hurt. Dad just told us both to stand where we were and it was not too long before we were smarting under the effects of the punishment we both knew we deserved. Yes, we were learning that God's law really made sense. Parents know best in most situations and God commands children to obey their parents in the Lord.

I imagine that most of my young readers have been brought up in Christian families. If so, you know about the Lord Jesus Christ. You have been taken to church and probably attend Sunday school. Even though you may not yet be a Christian, you know that God has commanded you to obey your parents and those who care for you.

May God bless all of you with parents who love Christ and always want the best for you, not only as far as the things of the world are concerned, but especially as far as spiritual matters are concerned. But even if you are not part of a Christian family, you still have a God-given responsibility to obey your mum and dad.

May God bless all the young people who have been reading these words. Some of my stories may bring a smile to your faces, but obedience to God is no laughing matter. May God make all my young readers good family members, obeying your parents 'in the Lord'.

Our Bible reading for today tells mums and dads what they, for their part, must do for their children — they must teach them the ways of God.

To think about
● ●

1. People who care for children have great responsibilities. List some of these responsibilities.
2. Why should children obey their parents? Is there any situation where a child might have to say, 'No, I can't do what you ask.' List some of those situations.
3. Describe what makes a happy Christian family.

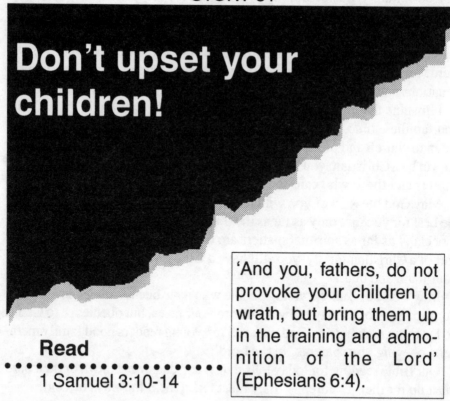

Don't upset your children!

Read
• • • • • • • • • • • • • • • • • • •
1 Samuel 3:10-14

'And you, fathers, do not provoke your children to wrath, but bring them up in the training and admonition of the Lord' (Ephesians 6:4).

All parents need to have time for their children. We must show our children and grandchildren that we really love them and want to help them at all times. This does not mean that we have to agree with all that our children do. It does not mean that at times we are not to tell them that we are upset with their behaviour. But it does mean that we are to be there for them and ready to help whenever we can. We are to do only those things that are

pleasing to God and our children must understand this. God must be honoured in every part of our lives and this is one of the means by which we instruct our children in the ways of the Lord. We need to be there to listen and to help our children in whatever ways we can.

Many years ago one of my daughters, who was in the senior part of the secondary school, came and

told me she had a part in a school play. I told her how pleased I was and she said I could read the play. It was a play about wartime and was to be acted before an audience in the local town hall. The play was put on my desk and that was where I left it. I didn't make time to read it.

A month or so later I saw a copy of the play lying on a table, picked it up and began reading. I was shocked to find that there was swearing in it and that in places the soldiers were mocked even though so many of them were injured and killed defending our democratic way of life. I was horrified that my daughter was involved in such a play. The next morning I called her aside and told her that she was not to take part in the play and that I would speak to her teacher about the matter.

She was very upset by what I said and replied, 'Dad, I gave you the play to read a month ago. That was when you should have said something. Please don't do anything now. We've learned our parts and if you say anything I'll be very embarrassed.'

I felt very uncomfortable!

Later that day I contacted the secondary school and, speaking to the master in charge of English teaching, explained the situation. He then investigated the matter for me. He was a Christian and unaware of the particular play being put on.

That afternoon when my daughter arrived home she burst into tears and said, 'I know it was you! The teacher came into the room and told us a parent had complained about the play and now we had to do something different.' I apologized again, but was taught a valuable lesson: take notice of what children say. I had caused a daughter much heartache which could have been avoided if only I had taken the time and trouble to look at the play when she first showed it to me.

We laugh about the incident now, but I know that my daughter takes notice of what her children say to her. She has learned from my mistake. I provoked my daughter to anger and tears by being thoughtless. She has forgiven me, but it should never have happened.

Parents, let us train our children in the ways of the Lord. We must encourage them, guide them and pray for them that early in life they may come to know Christ as their Saviour. Never let us be like Eli of old who did not take the trouble to correct his children. They died for their sins and poor Eli saw his sons die while he was still alive. The death of his godless children caused Eli much heartache. May we take godly Hannah as an example of how to deal with our children. She willingly gave her firstborn to serve the Lord.

May God grant all parents wisdom as they care for their children.

To think about
• •

1. Do you think parents are being kind when they punish you for breaking rules? Give reasons for your answer.
2. People who care for children should not deliberately do things to anger the children. What is meant by the words: 'Fathers, do not provoke your children to wrath'?
3. In what ways can parents teach their children about Christ and godly living?

Christmas always first

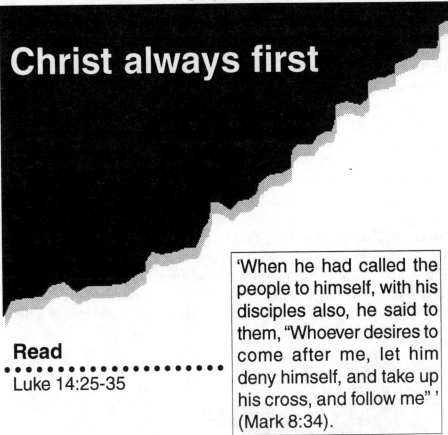

Read
• • • • • • • • • • • • • • • •
Luke 14:25-35

'When he had called the people to himself, with his disciples also, he said to them, "Whoever desires to come after me, let him deny himself, and take up his cross, and follow me" ' (Mark 8:34).

People sometimes have the idea that ministers only work on Sunday. I can assure you that ministers who take their responsibilities seriously work long hours. Preparations must be made for worship services, and this is to be done every week. There are people to be visited, the sick to be helped, the telephone to be answered, the dying to be comforted, long hours spent in prayer for the congregation — as well as in many cases the normal responsibilities of a husband and a father. Sometimes ministers are called out during the night to visit the dying and they often have to carry out many other jobs that most people know nothing about.

All Christians should know what it means to deny themselves as they follow Christ. Jesus said his people were to take up their cross and follow him. In New Testament times if you were told to take up your cross it meant that at the end of the road you would be nailed to it. As far as  Christians are concerned Christ must come first, and this can be difficult at times.

A pastor I know learned the hard way that Christ and his service must always have priority. He had spent the day driving around, visiting members of his congregation. He had visited several people in the local hospital as well as a few who were in homes for senior citizens. He had had a busy day and was looking forward to getting home, sitting down and having a meal with his wife and children.

 He arrived home later than he expected, but his family joyfully greeted him, giving him a cup of tea while he relaxed before the evening meal. Then the telephone rang. It was the wife of one of the men he had visited that morning in hospital. When the wife asked him to come at once as her husband had taken a turn for the worse, he assured the worried woman that he would be there as soon as possible.

Then he sat down and had his evening meal. He told his wife he had worked hard that day and deserved a little time with his family before he went to the hospital.

However, when he eventually arrived at the hospital he was met by a weeping woman who said that her husband had just passed away. Then she asked, 'Where were you? Bill wanted you to pray with him.'

That poor pastor went home distressed. If only he had left his meal until after he had made that visit to the hospital! He apologized to the lady and, taking the family aside, prayed with them, asking God to comfort them all in their grief. Then he went home, promising himself and the Lord that in future he would deny himself and daily take up his cross as he faithfully followed Christ.

The pastor had put his own comfort before the needs of a sick and dying man. It is so easy to put ourselves first. There are those times when we argue that a little comfort and pleasure comes before anything else — after all, we have earned it. But Jesus wants followers who are totally unselfish in the service they give him and his people. This means that all Christians must go out of their way to help others, especially those who are their brothers and sisters in Christ. We are to dedicate ourselves to the service of our Lord and Saviour Jesus Christ. He is to have the priority in our lives and self must always come last. If we are faithful servants of Christ, on Judgement Day we shall hear his words of praise: 'Well done, good and faithful servant... Enter into the joy of your Lord' (Matthew 25:23).

Our reading tells us that we must first count the cost involved in following Christ. If we are not willing to forsake everything for Christ we cannot be his disciples. There is an old chorus which teaches a great truth: 'Jesus first; yourself last; others in between!'

How do you stand with Christ? Are you a faithful servant who is willing to sacrifice all for him? Always remember that he gave everything that you might be saved. May God bless you as you serve our great Lord. Amen.

To think about
• •

1. At this period of your life what occupies most of your time? Is this how it should be?
2. Why should Christ always have the priority in our lives?
3. Whom will the Lord Jesus welcome with the words: 'Well done, good and faithful servant...'? (Matthew 25:23).
4. How can you show everyone that you are a Christian and that Christ is No. 1 in your life?

If you have read this book why not send a postcard of your homeland to me at the following address?

James A. Cromarty
3 Appaloosa Place
Wingham
N.S.W. 2429
Australia